S0-BHV-861

NEW YORK AND MID-ATLANTIC

Belhurst Castle, Geneva, New York

COUNTRY INNS OF AMERICA

New York

AND

Mid~Atlantic

A GUIDE TO THE INNS OF
NEW YORK, NEW JERSEY, PENNSYLVANIA, MARYLAND, AND VIRGINIA

BY ROBERTA HOMAN GARDNER

PHOTOGRAPHS BY GEORGE W. GARDNER

DESIGNED AND PRODUCED BY ROBERT R. REID
AND TERRY BERGER

An Owl Book

HENRY HOLT AND COMPANY

New York

Front cover: Delamater House at the Beekman Arms, Rhinebeck, New York.

Map: Anthony St. Aubyn.

Correspondence is welcome regarding the inns in this book, pro or con, and information about new inns not included should be mailed to: Robert Reid Associates, Apt. 5-D, University Towers, 100 York Street, New Haven, CT 06511.

Published by Henry Holt and Company, Inc., 521 Fifth Avenue, New York, New York 10175. Published simultaneously in Canada.

Library of Congress Cataloging-in-Publication Data

Gardner, Roberta Homan.
  New York and Mid-Atlantic : a guide to the inns of New York, New Jersey, Pennsylvania, Maryland, and Virginia.

  (Country inns of America)
  "An Owl book."
  Rev. ed. of: New York and Mid-Atlantic/Peter Andrews and Tracy Ecclesine. 1st ed. 1980.
  1. Hotels, taverns, etc.—Middle Atlantic States—Directories. I. Andrews, Peter, 1931– . New York and Mid-Atlantic. II. Title. III. Series.
TX907.G3425 1986   647'.947401   86-4641
ISBN 0-03-008517-9 (pbk.)
First Edition

10 9 8 7 6 5 4 3 2 1

A Robert Reid Associates Production
Typeset in Sabon Roman by Monotype Composition Company, Inc., Baltimore, Maryland
Printed and bound by Mandarin Offset Marketing (HK) Ltd.

ISBN 0-03-008517-9

THE INNS

Editor's Note

Country inns have come a long way since the first edition of this book was published. There are now many more inns in New York and the Mid-Atlantic states from which to choose those of the highest standards of food and décor. Such high levels of sophistication among more and more innkeepers have made it possible to produce a totally new, upscaled inn guide that will appeal to the most experienced inn-goer as well as attract new travelers to the wonderful world of country inns.

Since no two inns are alike, there is a good variety represented. Some are notable for their food, others for their restoration and furnishings, and still others for their historical and architectural interest. Some of course, are worth visiting because of their very special innkeepers.

Rather than give specific rates, which are always subject to change, we have designated rates as *inexpensive, moderate,* or *expensive.* This means that we consider

under $60 per double room as *inexpensive;*
$60 to $100 per double room as *moderate;*
over $100 per double room as *expensive.*

Since many inns now charge *per room,* rather than for singles or doubles, it would behoove single occupants to check rates carefully.

Some baths have both tub and shower, and some have only one or the other. If this concerns you, ask about it when talking to the innkeeper, as we have not taken the space to specify these details.

The word "daily" as we have used it means seven days a week, including weekends.

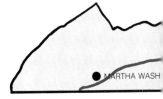

MARTHA WASH

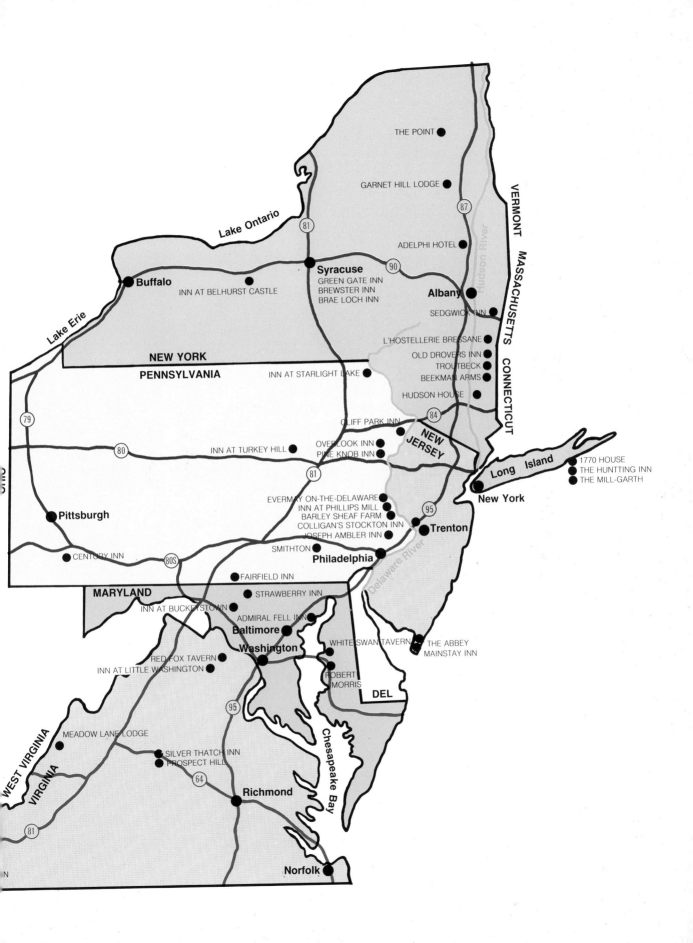

THE POINT ●

GARNET HILL LODGE ●

Lake Ontario
⑧¹

ADELPHI HOTEL ●

VERMONT
MASSACHUSETTS
CONNECTICUT

⑧⁷

Hudson River

Buffalo ●
●Syracuse
GREEN GATE INN
BREWSTER INN
BRAE LOCH INN

INN AT BELHURST CASTLE ●

⑨⁰

Lake Erie

Albany ●

SEDGWICK INN ●

L'HOSTELLERIE BRESSANE ●
OLD DROVERS INN ●
TROUTBECK ●
BEEKMAN ARMS ●

HUDSON HOUSE ●

NEW YORK
PENNSYLVANIA

INN AT STARLIGHT LAKE ●

CLIFF PARK INN ●

NEW
JERSEY

⑧⁴

⑦⁹

INN AT TURKEY HILL ●

OVERLOOK INN ●
PINE KNOB INN ●

Long   Island

1770 HOUSE ●
THE HUNTTING INN ●
THE MILL-GARTH ●

⑧⁰

New York ●

⑧¹

Pittsburgh ●

EVERMAY ON-THE-DELAWARE ●
INN AT PHILLIPS MILL ●
BARLEY SHEAF FARM ●
COLLIGAN'S STOCKTON INN ●
JOSEPH AMBLER INN ●

⑨⁵

Trenton ●

SMITHTON ●

⑧⁰ˢ
CENTURY INN ●

Philadelphia ●

Delaware River

FAIRFIELD INN ●

MARYLAND

STRAWBERRY INN ●

INN AT BUCKEYSTOWN ●

ADMIRAL FELL INN ●

Baltimore ●

WHITE SWAN TAVERN ● ● THE ABBEY
MAINSTAY INN

Washington ●

RED FOX TAVERN ●
INN AT LITTLE WASHINGTON ●

ROBERT
MORRIS ●

DEL

⑨⁵

Chesapeake Bay

WEST VIRGINIA
VIRGINIA

MEADOW LANE LODGE ●

SILVER THATCH INN ●
PROSPECT HILL ●

⑥⁴

Richmond ●

⑧¹

Norfolk ●

OHIO

NEW YORK

INN AT BELHURST CASTLE

Geneva   **NEW YORK**

Maureen's Room, with bonnet canopied bed and staircase to private balcony.

Finger Lakes nobility

Inns that garner the unbounded respect and recommendation of other innkeepers are a great find. The Inn at Belhurst Castle is one of these. It is a red Medina stone edifice which rests nobly at the edge of the crystal waters of Seneca Lake, the deepest of all New York's Finger Lakes. It was built in 1885 by Mrs. Carrie Harron Collins, who hired fifty craftsmen at a cost of nearly one-half million dollars.

Upon entering, past a sturdy porte cochère and through leaded-glass doors, one is immediately struck by the grand hallway's massive, crescent-shaped hearth—its face a patterned mosaic tile—and by the exquisitely detailed woodwork in cherry, olivewood, chestnut, white oak, and white Honduras mahogany.

Each of the guest rooms is handsomely appointed, and several are spectacular. The latter include Bob's Room, named for innkeeper Robert Golden; Maureen's Room with a canopied bed and private balcony; and the Tower Suite, a gigantic honeymoon paradise, complete with a private balcony overlooking the lake, a winding staircase that leads to the top of one of the castle's turrets, and a wood-paneled bathroom fitted with a capacious Jacuzzi tub.

The Dwyer Suite is spacious and comfortable enough to prompt thoughts of a long, leisurely stay. The suite's bedroom offers a massive four-poster-bed, the adjoining living room, a warming fire, and from each, a view through elegant stained-glass windows of the inn's garden, which runs to the shore of Seneca Lake. To toast the scene, guests find just outside the door a spigot from which flows an endless supply of white wine.

The entire first floor of the inn comprises a series of dining rooms and a wood-paneled taproom. As one might imagine, this spectacular setting attracts a large number of diners, but the quality of workmanship in the building is such that sound does not carry past the foyer. Three meals are served daily in the inn's dining rooms, and the dinner menu features classic treatments of seafood, fowl, and meat, with the addition of several "nouvelle" American dishes.

Above, sitting room of the Dwyer Suite. *Left*, ornate mosaic tile and carved wood fireplace in the entry hall. *Previous pages*, the lawn, gardens, and castle overlooking Seneca Lake.

THE INN AT BELHURST CASTLE, Lochland Road, P.O. Box 609, Geneva, NY 14456; (315) 781-0201; Bob Golden, Innkeeper. Rates: *moderate* and *expensive*. Open all year; 10 rooms and 2 suites, all with private baths. Restaurant serves 3 meals every day to guests and public; Sunday brunch; liquor served. Children welcome; no pets; French spoken; major credit cards accepted. Golfing, swimming, rod and reel fishing, boating, waterskiiing, wineries, antiquing, Alpine and Nordic skiing.

DIRECTIONS: from I-90 take Geneva exit 42 south for 8 miles on Rte. 14. Arrange for pickup in Rochester for plane and Syracuse for train.

An inn restored from old photographs

For nearly the first eighty years of its existence, the Green Gate Inn was a private home. Then in 1939, an enterprising soul named Bertha Carrington bought the house and opened what was to become a thriving and popular restaurant. By the 1980s Bertha was long gone and the 1861 building well past its prime; yet the memory of the inn's earlier days lingered in the minds of local inhabitants. When Dan and Linda Roche discovered that the old Green Gate was for sale, they decided it was time to give the inn a new life. For years Dan had worked as a master carpenter

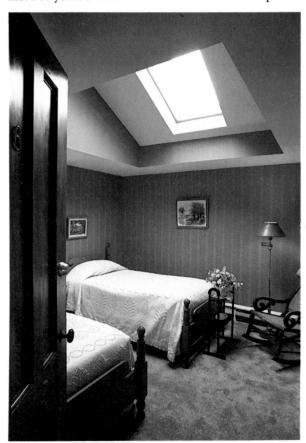

and talented jack-of-all-trades, renovating other people's homes. The inn offered him at last a chance to work for himself. Dan began the formidable task of refurbishing the comfortable Victorian structure by studying old photographs in order to reproduce its original roof lines, cornices, and trim. The Roches have invested such love and care in their inn that first-time visitors came away feeling that they've stumbled upon a missing branch of the family.

Among Dan's most notable achievements is the inn's bar. He not only designed the room and its detailed woodwork but also selected trees for the lumber, supervised their milling, and fully constructed the handsome, inviting tavern. The bar serves light meals and complimentary snacks during happy hour. Nearby a satisfying array of treats awaits diners in the inn's formal dining rooms. The Green Gate's reputation as a fine restaurant is rapidly growing, thanks to such fare as fresh sole sautéed with leeks, pecans and lime, and crispy, boneless breast of duck stuffed with black currants and pecans and coated with glistening black currant sauce.

Above, Room 6, with skylight. *Left*, Linda and Dan Roche, innkeepers, in the Green Gate taproom, designed and built entirely by Dan.

GREEN GATE INN, 2 Main Street, Camillus, NY 13031; (315) 672-9276; Linda and Dan Roche and Dan Jr., Innkeepers. Rates: *inexpensive* and *moderate*, including generous continental breakfast. Open all year; 6 rooms, all with private baths, 3 with Jacuzzis, 1 with steam sauna. Restaurant open for lunch and dinner daily except Mondays, to guests and public; tavern menu for other meals; liquor served. No pets; no smoking in guest rooms; Visa, MasterCard, American Express accepted. Golf, tennis, swimming, riding, nature trails, wineries, Finger Lakes boat tours.

DIRECTIONS: from I-90 take exit 39 to Rte. 690 to Camillus exit. Turn left and go 2 blocks to Rte. 5 (Main Street). Turn left and drive 2 blocks to inn. Arrange for pickup in Syracuse for train or plane.

The inn has a waterfront view of Lake Cazenovia.

A lakeside mansion with classic cooking

In the late 1700s, the first settlers arrived along the banks of Lake Cazenovia, drawn by the beauty of the rolling hillsides. Within a century the area was attracting the successful and wealthy who built summer homes along the shore. Foremost among this privileged group was Benjamin B. Brewster, who chose one of the loveliest spots along the lakeside as the site of his home. He spared no expense in creating an elegant summer mansion, which he dubbed "Scrooby" after the English manor house of his forebearer William Brewster who had set out with the Pilgrims for the New World.

By the early 1980s Benjamin Brewster's summer retreat was bought by Dick and Cathy Hubbard, who opened it to the public as The Brewster Inn. Dick had had more than a decade's experience managing successful inns in the Finger Lakes district before deciding to strike out on his own. Because of his innate understanding of hospitality, excellent management, and good sense of humor, this fledging inn already stands out from the crowd.

To reach the bedrooms on the second and third floors of the house, guests ascend a curving, formal staircase, with a deeply coffered ceiling overhead and thick Oriental rugs underfoot. Master bedrooms on the second floor are the largest rooms in the inn. Room 2 contains an especially fine, matched walnut bedroom set of Eastlake design, and Room 1, set into one of the house's many bays, overlooks the manicured lawn and lakefront. Whether in these stately quarters or in the charming third-floor garrets, guests will find their accommodations filled with character and with all the comforts they might wish.

The Brewster Inn's dining room offers delicious fare that ranges from simple to classic and includes such enticing choices as gallantine of duck with raspberry sauce; escargots en croûte; sautéed pork tenderloin nestled in a sauce of reduced cream, brandy, and crushed peppercorns; broiled lamb chops in hazelnut sauce; and a thick cut prime rib of beef with horseradish sauce and Yorkshire pudding. All breads are baked in the kitchen, and it takes an act of will to resist the urge for just one more hot and yeasty dinner roll.

Above, Room 4 overlooks the lake from the top floor. *Left*, main entrance hall, with its impressively coffered ceiling.

THE BREWSTER INN, Rte. 20, Cazenovia, NY 13035; (315) 655-9232; Dick and Cathy Hubbard, Innkeepers. Rates: *inexpensive* and *moderate*, including continental breakfast. Open all year; 8 rooms with private baths. Restaurant serves dinner all year to guests and public, and lunch in summer; liquor served. Children welcome; no pets; all major credit cards accepted. Golfing, tennis, swimming, sailing, fishing, antiquing, Nordic skiing.

DIRECTIONS: take I-81 south to Rte. 20 and go east to Cazenovia. Watch for sign on left before entering village. Arrange for pickup at Syracuse for train or plane.

BRAE LOCH INN

Cazenovia   **NEW YORK**

A Scottish inn run by the clan

To residents of central New York the Brae Loch Inn is a well-loved institution. To travelers along scenic route 20 the Brae Loch is a surprise; a Scottish inn in the center of New York State's orchard, vineyard, and lake country. Innkeeper and master of hospitality Grey Barr has owned and operated this inn since 1949, and his natural ebullience attracts more than devoted guests. Today he is in the enviable position of employing the majority of his six children. Together they imbue the Brae Loch with a familial warmth and harmony.

The inn sits on a prominent corner, at the edge of Cazenovia's charming main street and across from Cazenovia Lake. The large brown frame structure, dressed up with shingles and sky blue shutters, doesn't hint at the tiny piece of Scotland that resides within. Visitors are drawn first to the Brae Loch's colorful gift shop filled with a variety of goods, from candies and cards to soaps and toys, but featuring fine Scottish imports such as kilts, sweaters, ties, and tams. Wandering along the first floor, past the entry parlor with hearth and life-size carved and painted Scottish laddie, one discovers the inn's formal dining rooms, used on weekends, with their striking red flocked wallpaper, gold velvet drapes, and Victorian tufted velvet dining chairs. Downstairs are the dining rooms that are used seven days a week. Here plaid carpeting, deep red

Innkeeper H. Grey Barr in formal tartan dress.

table cloths, symbols of Scotland, and wood paneling blend together to create a casual and warm mood.

The quiet top floor of the inn is devoted to guest bedrooms, and the 1805 section of the house accommodates four of the most old-fashioned of the twelve. Princess Diana is appropriately feminine and frilly with a canopied bed dripping with white eyelet. Queen Elizabeth, across the hall, encloses a king-size canopied bed and blends patterns and patchwork in warm shades of burgundy, brown, and cream. Proceeding down the hallway one passes comfortable chambers added as the inn grew.

Above, Room 4, named after Princess Diana. *Left*, the richly appointed sitting room, *top*, and the inviting dining room, *bottom*.

BRAE LOCH INN, 5 Albany Street (Rte. 20), Cazenovia, NY 13035; (315) 655-3431; H. Grey and Doris Barr and family, Innkeepers. Rates: *moderate* and *expensive*, including continental breakfast. Open all year; 12 rooms with private baths. Restaurant serves dinner every day to guests and public, and special Sunday brunch; liquor served. Children welcome; no pets, all major credit cards accepted. Golf, tennis, boating, swimming, New York state's largest antiques show in mid-August, Alpine skiing.

DIRECTIONS: from Lafayette off I-81 take Rte. 20 east 15 miles to Cazenovia. Proceed past blinker light to first stoplight and turn left to inn. Arrange pickup in Syracuse (20 miles) for train or plane.

Rockefeller's spectacular mountain retreat

In the early 1930s William Avery Rockefeller happened upon a set of blueprints in the office of William G. Distin, Adirondack camp architect *par excellence*. The blueprints revealed a spectacular mountain retreat, an estate so striking he demanded to know for whom Distin was working. Distin explained there was no client. He had designed a "folly," a dream camp far too extravagant to ever realize. To make a long story short, Rockefeller told him that he had to have it. After searching for the perfect site, which turned out to be a nine-acre promontory overlooking pristine Saranac Lake, Rockefeller and Distin built the finest Adirondack camp in existence. By early 1980 this camp, known as The Point and owned by Ted Carter and Jim Myhre, opened its doors to paying houseguests.

It is difficult to classify The Point as a country inn, *Left,* the main lodge. *Below*, the Great Hall, with its many mounted trophies, its blazing fire, and relaxing atmosphere.

per se, because it is really a rustic and sophisticated private home to which congenial guests are most welcome.

Upon arrival you are shown to your room, which might include a walk-in sized stone fireplace or a bed suspended on a balcony overlooking the lake. Each guest room has a custom-made bed and down comforter, plush robes, and other thoughtful details meant to pamper. After settling in, a tour of this compound, which includes a boathouse and a clutch of rustic out-cabins, beckons. The Great Hall, with its twenty-foot cathedral ceiling, two massive hewn-stone hearths, and knotless pine paneling (each piece the center plank from its parent log) is the focal point of the main lodge and is furnished with a grand array of antiques, twig chairs, mounted game trophies, commodious buffalo plaid sofas, and tables ready for the evening repast. There is even an antique Old Town canoe perched high amidst the rafters.

A day at The Point begins with a basket of baked goods delivered to each room. Afterwards guests are free to tour the lake via one of eight craft (not including the fleet of antique mahogany speedboats fit for the Great Gatsby, which only Ted or Jim may

captain), or take a brisk hike through pristine wilderness. Lunch is a free-wheeling affair that might take place on a neighboring island or tucked before a crackling fire. In summer, the before-dinner cocktail hour often convenes on the boathouse barge which tours the shoreline while guests get to know each other. At day's end, the evening meal is prepared by Jim, who has gained a reputation for culinary finesse, and is presided over with style by Ted, who is an urbane host and world-class raconteur.

THE POINT, Star Route, Saranac Lake, NY 12983; (518) 891-5674; Ted Carter, Innkeeper. Rates: *very expensive*, including continental breakfast, lunch, dinner, and 24-hour bar; special winter rates. Open all year; 9 rooms in lodge and cottage, all with private baths. Dining room open every day for guests only. Children over 11 welcome during winter season (Nov. 1 to end of April); pets welcome; French spoken; American Express accepted. Croquet, badminton, boating, tennis, golf, health club with sauna, ice skating, ice fishing, Nordic skiing.

DIRECTIONS: sent upon receipt of confirmed reservation.

Opposite page, innkeeper Ted Carter in one of his vintage speedboats, a gleaming Hacker Craft c. 1929. *Below*: the room Weatherwatch in the separate Clifftop Lodge, dominated by the huge stone hearth. *Right*, entrance hall of the Main Lodge, hung with Carter family memorabilia.

A classic Adirondack hideaway

Rear view of Log House, the main lodge.

Entering Garnet Hill's main lodge, aptly named Log House for its full timber beams and support columns, guests immediately relax. Amidst such rustic surroundings and unpretentious warmth it is nearly impossible to hold onto any vestige of worry or care. This atmosphere is due in great part to the genial spirit of innkeepers George and Mary Heim, who operate Garnet Hill with a light, sure touch. While George tends to affairs in the front of the house, Mary presides over the kitchen; and the balance they strike is perfect. The lodge itself is also largely responsible for the ambience. This is a classic Adirondack hideaway with a large hearth built from massive stones flecked with shiny fragments of garnet, which has been mined for years from the surrounding mountains.

Guests are given every opportunity to build a hearty appetite during a visit to Garnet Hill. Adjoining the 50,000-acre Siamese Pond Wilderness Area and sitting atop a mountain that overlooks sparkling 13th Lake, the inn offers a seemingly endless variety of outdoor activities geared to every level of energy and ability. Summer guests enjoy boating, swimming in the lake, or sunning on the inn's private, sand beach. Fall foliage in these parts is nothing short of spectacular, and the inn's cross-country ski facilities—complete with instructors, equipment, and state-of-the-

art trail-grooming equipment—are second to none. Hiking enthusiasts, fishermen, hunters, or city folks starved for crisp, clean air and miles of untouched wilderness find seventh heaven at Garnet Hill.

After working up a sharp appetite, guests will find Mary's cooking saves the day. After starting with a breakfast of griddle cakes and maple syrup or French toast made with thick slabs of homemade bread, one might lunch on delicious homemade soup and sandwiches. Even light eaters discover that a day in the Adirondacks allows plenty of room for Mary's simple, but satisfying dinners, which accommodate the full gamut of tastes and appetites. Two special entrées are featured each evening as well as the menu's selection of fish, fowl, chops, and steaks. Garnet Hill has a reputation for wonderful baked goods made fresh daily, including yeast and batter breads, cookies, brownies, and flaky pies, all of which will test the will of even the most ardent of dieters.

Above, 13th Lake, good for boating, fishing, and swimming from its sand beach. *Left,* the garnet-flecked fireplace in the sitting room of the main lodge, *top,* and some of the delicious baking for which the inn is known, *bottom.*

GARNET HILL LODGE, 13th Lake Road, North River, NY 12856; (518) 251-2821; George and Mary Heim, Innkeepers. Rates: *moderate,* European plan or modified American plan. Open all year except for 2 weeks at Thanksgiving and 2 weeks in June; 25 rooms (Main Lodge 14, Ski Haus 1, Big Shanty 6, The Birches 4) with private baths except Big Shanty, which shares 4 baths. Dining room serves 3 meals every day, plus special Saturday Smorgasbord, to inn guests only; liquor served. Children welcome; no pets; checks accepted, no credit cards. Tennis, billiards, ping pong, fishing, swimming from sand beach, Alpine skiing, Nordic skiing with groomed trails, ski shop, and instructors.

DIRECTIONS: from I-87 take exit 23 on Rtes. 9/28 north 4 miles to fork in road. Take Rte. 28, 22 miles to North River. Take 2nd left onto 13th Lake Rd. 5 miles to lodge.

ADELPHI HOTEL

Saratoga Springs   **NEW YORK**

An opulent reflection of Saratoga's romantic past

Motoring along the length of Broadway, the main street of Saratoga Springs, travelers are captivated by the sophisticated charm of its shops and restaurants, and its distinctive turn-of-the-century character. Throughout the late nineteenth century, when Saratoga was one of the most fashionable spas in the country, the cream of society descended en masse each summer to take the waters and enjoy America's finest thoroughbred racing. Broadway was lined with opulent hotels that housed this glittering throng; The Adelphi Hotel was among the crown jewels of that golden era. Today, in the care of innkeepers Gregg Siefker and Sheila Parkert, The Adelphi is in renascence. It is a grand reflection of Saratoga's romantic, Victorian hotels.

Left, innkeeper Sheila Parkert at the check-in desk. *Below,* the hotel fronts on Broadway, Saratoga's main street.

The façade of the hotel, colored in rich shades of brown, cream, green, and rust, is an Italian villa-style concoction composed of towering columns, intricate fretwork, a second-story, wicker-filled piazza, and tall, slender windows. The lobby is dark and lush: four central wood columns create a private space furnished with period sofas and arm chairs dressed in rich brocades and satins. Antique plant stands display dramatic sprays of flowers, and potted palms shelter private conversation areas. Soft celery green swags frame the entry to the hotel's café bar which is furnished with upholstered banquettes and cream satin brocade walls. In July and August, luncheon, followed by a light supper served until midnight, is available in the café and adjoining open-air garden. During high summer, which heralds the height of Saratoga's bustling "season," The Adelphi also opens its elegant supper club. Sheila is an accomplished chef and she prepares such dishes as duck breast with pungent black currant sauce and grilled filet of beef served with a roquefort, horseradish, scallion cream sauce. Throughout the spring and fall seasons the kitchen is closed for lunch and dinner, and The Adelphi is hushed and relaxed. Saratoga, free of the summer throng, is yours to explore and enjoy.

Gregg and Sheila work in tandem restoring and decorating the hotel. A broad, four-story central staircase leads guests to bedchambers and carries the eye to the large ceiling window that washes the interior with light. On each level, broad and tall hallways are furnished with statuary, settees, crazy quilt wallhangings, and prints. Many of the accommodations are two-room suites, and all are lavishly and romantically decorated and comfortably furnished.

THE ADELPHI HOTEL, 365 Broadway, Saratoga Springs, NY 12866; (518) 587-4688; Gregg Siefker and Sheila Parkert, Innkeepers. Rates: *moderate* off season, *expensive* during August, including continental breakfast. Open May through November; 25 rooms including 10 suites, all with private baths. Restaurant open to guests and public for dinner only during July and August, Thursday to Sunday. Café serves lunch and dinner Wednesday to Sunday; liquor served all days. Children welcome; pets welcome; Visa, MasterCard, American Express accepted. Saratoga Performing Arts Center is home of New York City Ballet during July and Philadelphia Orchestra during August. Saratoga races during August.

DIRECTIONS: I-87 to Saratoga Springs; all 3 exits end up in center of town, where hotel is on Broadway, the town's main street.

Opposite page, The Adelphi's gilded lobby. *Below left*, breakfast is delivered to your room on a silver tray. *Below right*, Room 27, with lavender moiré silk walls, is wildly romantic. *Right*, Room 22 has a fine-grained wooden bed accented with a colonial Jacquard coverlet.

SEDGWICK INN

Berlin   **NEW YORK**

Congenial hosts with a flair for food

Innkeeper Bob Evans. Entry to the wine cellar is at left, where guests may choose their wine for a meal.

There are just a small handful of country inns filled with the kind of special good spirits that spring from a history of congenial people and happy times. The Sedgwick surely ranks among them. Decades ago that arbiter of good eating, Duncan Hines, gave the inn his seal of approval. He would reissue the same if he were on the road today. From the outside the inn is one of New England's classic white clapboard rambling structures; the kind of place that looks worn and comfortable and eminently inviting. Inside an overall lack of pretension allows visitors to relax and breathe a sigh of contentment. Innkeepers Bob and Edie Evans value this spirit and mean to sustain it. Both were professionals in the mental health field who decided to take up new careers in this not totally unrelated occupation.

Though retired from social work, Edie, originally from Vienna, remains a gifted sculptor who turns a good deal of her creative energies toward culinary pursuits. As a result the Sedgwick kitchen is gaining a fine reputation and steadfast following. The dining room has age-burnished wooden floors, old-fashioned patterned wallpaper, mix and match wooden dining tables, each graced with a single rose. The evening's repast might feature veal saltimbocca, chicken with plum sauce, Merry Olde Sole (two filets of lemon sole sautéed and baked with shrimp, crab, and mozzarella cheese), or Schwartzenburg pot roast. Though Edie is known for the tempting soups she concocts,

she receives accolades for inspired desserts such as almond torte with lemon sherbet, raspberry bavarian, and an especially successful frozen chocolate mousse pie. Diners also enjoy journeying into the wine cellar to choose their bottle from an inventory which carries astonishingly low price tags.

Bob's special area of interest is collecting antiques that fill the entire inn and spill over into the inn's antique shops, one of which was a Civil War recruiting station dating to 1834. His collections add warmth to the inn's charming library and living room, where a small group of Edie's stone sculpture is displayed. The four bedrooms on the second floor of the inn are filled with an eclectic collection of antique beds and chests, while the motel-like units at the rear of the property are furnished simply with lace curtains, comfortable beds, and miscellaneous chairs and bureaus. Good reading is a priority with these innkeepers and interesting material is found in every room in the inn.

Above, Room 7 accommodates antique brass cannonball twin beds. *Left,* guests relax on the lawn adjoining the inn's restaurant at the back.

THE SEDGWICK INN, Rte. 22, Berlin, NY 12022; (518) 658-2334; Bob and Edie Evans, Innkeepers. Rates: *moderate*, including full breakfast. Open all year except for November and 2 weeks in April; 10 rooms including 4 in inn. Restaurant serves 2 meals a day to guests and public; closed Monday in summer, Monday and Tuesday in winter; liquor served. Children and pets by special arrangement; no smoking in guest rooms, no cigars and pipes in dining room; German and French spoken; all major credit cards accepted. Summer theater, Clark Museum, golf, tennis in Williamstown (15 miles); Tanglewood (25 minutes); Bennington, Vt. (19 miles).

DIRECTIONS: on Rte. 22 between Stephentown and Petersburg, N.Y. No charge for pickup at Albany airport.

L'HOSTELLERIE BRESSANE

Hillsdale   **NEW YORK**

The haven of a great chef

Jean Morel isn't just a good chef, he is a great chef. Devotees of his fine auberge, L'Hostellerie Bressane, think nothing of driving hours to enjoy the artistry of his table. Those lucky few who secure overnight reservations may drink and dine to satisfaction, knowing they will also enjoy a comfortable night's sleep in a beautiful Dutch Colonial inn.

To maintain a reputation such as Chef Morel's takes genuine dedication, energy and love and is, in his words, "a nonstop struggle to stay ahead of the pack." To the joy of his guests, Chef Moral excels at this struggle and makes it look easy. His light, classical cuisine features the freshest of ingredients from the most reliable suppliers. Bresse chicken, fresh game, prime cuts of meat, and seafoods such as lotte, live crayfish, and fresh salmon find their way into dishes such as hot duck pâté in puff pastry served with poivrade sauce; duck raviolis in a cream sauce with chives; crayfish Bordelaise; chicken with crayfish Nantual; and fresh salmon with tomato butter sauce. All desserts, including light and creamy soufflés, sherbets, and ice creams, are made in the kitchen; and presentations are almost too lovely to disturb. Guests should take time to peruse the inn's wine list; Chef Morel's cellar is filled with thoughtfully selected vintages.

The architecture of L'Hostellerie Bressane, which was built in 1782 and originally served as a coach

Chef Jean Morel.

stop, is pure colonial America. Once inside and greeted by charming châtelaine Madeleine Morel, however, diners are transported to the Morels' native province of Bresse, France. Hutches filled with lovely china, oil paintings, and three age-darkened hearths are accented by tables covered with crisp white tablecloths and topped with vases of fresh flowers. The six guest rooms are found on the second and third floors of the inn, the top floor housing the most deluxe chambers. There, one bedroom named Lavender offers a treetop view of the grounds through a graceful Palladian window.

Above, a façade of the inn, although not the main entrance. *Left*, Chef Morel's succulent creations are beautifully presented.

L'HOSTELLERIE BRESSANE, Hillsdale, NY 12529; (518) 325-3412; Jean and Madeleine Morel, Innkeepers. Rates: *moderate*. Open all year except March and April; 6 rooms with private and shared baths. Dinner only served to guests and public 5 days a week, Wednesday through Sunday; liquor served. Children welcome; no pets; French and Spanish spoken; no commercial credit cards accepted—inn issues own card. Nearby Berkshires provide year-round activities: summer theater, Tanglewood, Jacob's Pillow Dance Festival, skiing, antiquing.

DIRECTIONS: on east side of Hudson River, near Massachusetts border, at the intersection of Rtes. 22 and 23.

A retreat for lovers of natural beauty

Innkeeper Jim Flaherty suspects Troutbeck is touched by magic. It does have an uncanny ability to draw an amazing array of people and wonderful things happen. Its history includes guests like Sinclair Lewis, Lewis Mumford, naturalist John Burroughs, President Teddy Roosevelt, and W.E.B. DuBois as well as such events as the founding under its roof of the N.A.A.C.P.

Perhaps it's the setting that provides inspiration. The grounds encompass 400 acres and form the crossroads of a broad river and a babbling brook, along which stands a stately row of towering sycamore trees. John Burroughs assisted nature with additional plantings of trees and flowers that enhance the sweet harmony of this graceful piece of land. To replace the original 1790 structure, which had burned to the ground in 1914, a Tudor-style manor house was constructed with shaggy slate roof, rough stone, and leaded windows. Though the existing home is large and rambling, it feels both intimate and imbued with a spirit of enchantment.

Troutbeck is open to inn-goers from Friday through Sunday and during the week serves as what Jim calls "the gold standard of executive retreats." Weekend guests are treated to an intimate atmosphere that seems more like a friend's weekend home than a hostelry. Because the inn was built as a private residence, guest bedrooms in the manor house are not at all standardized. One might choose to stay in the master suite, complete with canopied bed, working fireplace, and private enclosed porch, or in a hideaway tucked into the eaves. On the opposite bank of the Webatuck River is the Century Farmhouse, which also contains guest rooms—several in the original house dating to the mid-1700s and the remainder in a brand-new wing designed to complement the colonial farmhouse.

Weekend guests dine exquisitely. Before dinner, they help themselves from the tea-cart bar, which is reminiscent of home and sets the mood for a totally relaxing evening. The inn's gifted chefs are given free

Left, top, Troutbeck's sumptuous living room, looking toward the Red Room and the open bar. *Bottom,* the dining room, washed with light, overlooks a rock garden and trout pond. *Overleaf,* Troutbeck's main house, a Tudor mansion straight out of a fairytale, with its shaggy slate roof and leaded glass windows.

A comfortable guest room in the main house.

reign to create the most pleasing and memorable of culinary delights, all served in the intimate sun porch-dining room, which overlooks a well-tended rock garden and tranquil trout pond. A limited menu—which might include tournedos with a green peppercorn, raisin, and brandy sauce; baby lemon sole meuniere; and breast of capon with wild mushrooms and armagnac—allows Troutbeck's kitchen the luxury of perfect execution.

TROUTBECK, Box 26, Leedsville Road, Amenia, NY 12501; (914) 373-9681; Jim Flaherty, Innkeeper. Rates: *very expensive,* including full breakfast, full lunch, 5 course dinner, and open bar. Open all year; 26 rooms with private baths. Dining room open to public on weekends. Children under 1 and over 12 welcome; no pets; smoking but no cigars in dining room; Spanish, Portuguese, Italian, and French spoken; American Express accepted. Swimming, sauna, exercise room, volleyball, tennis, badminton, video movies, poker table, 12,000 book library on premises; antiquing, golf, Roosevelt and Vanderbilt mansions nearby.

DIRECTIONS: provided upon reservation.

OLD DROVERS INN

Dover Plains **NEW YORK**

Authentic colonial atmosphere

When it comes to authentic colonial American atmosphere, the Old Drovers Inn sets the standard. The original tavern was built in 1750 by a pair of conservative Quaker brothers, John and Ebenezer Preston. Though the brothers disapproved of drinking and carousing, they were practical men at heart. When the inn became a popular stopover for the rowdy crowd of drovers, who shepherded livestock past this establishment en route from New York to New England, the Prestons turned a blind eye. They accommodated their guests' thirst by setting out a barrel of spirits and accepting whatever donations might come their way. This bit of innkeeping savvy proved successful, and the inn thrived.

This same accommodating spirit of innkeeping is alive and well at the Old Drovers today. The inn, owned by the Potter family since 1937 and now managed by Charles Wilbur, doesn't take to change, for which hundreds of Old Drovers addicts are eternally grateful. Here, uneven, irregular floorboards, doors, and walls are almost an art form. Guests ascend one floor to the clutch of bedchambers and are transported to the 1770s. The first bedroom in a collection of three is named the Sleigh Room and is furnished with an antique double sleigh bed, a vintage vanity, two wing chairs, and hook rugs. This room and its neighbor, the Cherry Room, are outfitted with ancient, working hearths that sport original colonial paneling. The Meeting Room, located around the corner and two steps down, is a favorite, with vaulted ceiling, working fireplace, and upholstered easy chairs with the inn's trademark, plump down cushions.

The main floor of the inn is the guests' domain, and many choose to spend time in the comfortable library with its vast collection of old tomes, inviting chairs and couches, and priceless shell wall hutch—whose mate resides in the American Wing of the Metropolitan Museum in New York City.

Left, top, the Library at Old Drovers. The shell case is one of a matched set whose mate is in the American Wing of the Metropolitan Museum of Art in New York City. *Bottom*, Open beams and a huge colonial hearth set the mood in the inn's dining room.

The totally captivating Meeting Room, with its irregular lines, vaulted ceiling, hearth, and overstuffed chintz wing chairs.

In the evening guests troop one flight down to the Old Drovers' long-established and well-loved dining room. The focal point here is a massive stone hearth surrounded by tables. The kitchen has long been known for its cheddar cheese soup, pâté of game bird livers, browned turkey hash with mustard sauce, and fruit cobbler made to order.

OLD DROVERS INN, Old Post Road, Dover Plains, NY 12522; (914) 832-9311; Charles Wilbur, Innkeeper, James Potter, Proprietor. Rates: *expensive*; 3 rooms with private baths. Open all year except for 3 weeks in December; closed Tuesday and Wednesday year round; rooms available Thursday through Sunday nights. Full breakfast served to inn guests only; lunch and dinner served to guests and public; liquor served. No pets; American Express accepted. Antiquing, artisans' craft village, Culinary Institute, Hyde Park nearby.

DIRECTIONS: located on Old Drover's Road, off Rte. 22, 4 miles north of Wingdale.

At the center of picturesque Rhinebeck

American history buffs and inn aficionados alike rarely find a richer environment in which to explore their interest than at the Beekman Arms, which sits at the center of picturesque Rhinebeck. Open before the Revolution and placed strategically along the Hudson River, a well-trodden route since the early 1700s, the inn has seen tumult, growth, and happy times.

Today's guest may choose to stay in the historic inn, perhaps in the very room where William Jennings Bryan orated from the second story balcony, or in one of several out buildings, each of which has its own character and appeal. Rooms in the original inn are old-fashioned, with irregular wooden floors, oval braid rugs, and a mix of antiques and colonial reproduction furnishings. Just one block away is the Delamater Guest House which was built in 1844 and is a beautiful example of American Carpenter Gothic architecture, with pointed roof line, decorative balcony and porch columns. and intricate diamond-paned windows.

Past the back door of the Delamater and along its wide sweep of lawn is the Delamater's Carriage House. Here, rooms are decorated in a more rustic mood, dictated by bits of rough open beamwork that shows through from the original structure. Behind

A cozy guest room in the Carriage House, with original exposed timbers and skylight.

the Carriage House, innkeeper Chuck La Forge recently added the Delamater Courtyard to the Beekman Arm's inventory of accommodations. Each of the rooms in the Courtyard are very fresh, modern, and luxurious but strive to maintain a simple country mood, using sprightly wallpapers and period furnishings, and stocking each working fireplace with an evening's worth of blazing good cheer. Finally, the centerpiece of the Courtyard is the Germond House, which was moved to this spot and completely renovated to include luxury suites.

As in centuries past, a continuous stream of humanity flows through the lobby of the inn, most people arriving to partake of the Beekman's classic cuisine. Staples such as prime ribs of beef, roast duckling, buttermilk pecan chicken, and veal with apples, cream, and calvados brandy are paired with the inn's popular new "country spa" menu in which no fats, salts, and sugars are used.

Above, guest rooms in the newest part of the inn are spacious and nicely detailed. *Left*, the original colonial inn, *top*, and the newer Courtyard, *bottom*, built in carpenter gothic style to match Delamater House, shown on the cover.

BEEKMAN ARMS, Rhinebeck NY 12572; (914) 876-7077; Charles LaForge, Innkeeper. Rates: *moderate*, including continental breakfast in Delamater complex. Open all year; 50 rooms with private baths, many with working fireplaces, in original colonial inn building and Delamater complex (comprised of original Victorian Gothic Delamater House, Carriage House, Courtyard, and Germond House). Restaurant serves 3 meals daily to guests and public; liquor served. Children welcome; pets welcome in colonial inn building only; all major credit cards accepted. Nearby tennis, golf, antiquing; most famous attraction is the Rhinebeck aerodrome, with antique WW I aeroplanes and air shows in summer and fall.

DIRECTIONS: Rte. 9 goes direct to Rhinebeck. Inn is in center of town.

Spic and span and thoroughly comfortable

Cold Spring, on the Hudson, is one of the most inviting of the many small villages that cluster along the banks of the Hudson River. The long Main Street sweeps to the banks of the river past old-fashioned houses and a commercial district filled with antiques and specialty shops. At the end of the street there is a large white gazebo, surrounded from late October to May by the river's resident flock of snowy swans. Immediately next to the gazebo sits the Hudson House, New York's second-oldest inn in continuous operation. Though its age is apparent, the inn wears it well; the completely refurbished Hudson House is spic and span and thoroughly comfortable. Innkeeper Mary Pat Sawyer, who for years was a dancer with the San Francisco Ballet, "retired" to the rigors of operating this popular hostelry. Her creative talent and unflagging energy permeate the inn, making for an appealing, interesting atmosphere.

Mary Pat has decorated the inn with an eye to revealing the clean and simple lines of the building. The lobby sitting room contains couches upholstered in a provencal red, white, and blue pattern with draperies in the reversed pattern. On the walls are displayed the works of local artists: a master clock-maker's one-of-a-kind work; a series of ethereal watercolors. Guest rooms, located on the second and third floors continue this refreshingly simple theme. Antique chests and wardrobes stripped down to their

The spacious lobby, with a display of handmade clocks by Herbert Keuchen.

natural finish, painted metal, wood, or brass bed frames, and dainty printed wallpapers predominate. Several rooms open onto decks that face the river, its neighboring dramatic cliffs, and the famous West Point, which juts dramatically toward the water just a short distance down river.

Mary Pat sees to it that her guests dine well and to that end has developed a menu grounded in early American cookery. The cold chicken breast salad with curry and chutney that appears on the luncheon menu is inspired; pasta with garden vegetables, country roast pork with apricots, nesting chicken, and lamb with pepper and tarragon sauce are dinnertime regulars. Desserts sound enticing—lemon cloud, country cream freeze, raspberry rapture, berries and Devonshire cream, orange delight. During clement weather dining on the porch while watching the Hudson roll by is a pleasure, and alfresco dining in a private garden tucked behind the inn is enjoyed throughout the summer.

Above, the simplicity and freshness of Room 1, which overlooks the river from the porch. *Left*, Hudson House and the village gazebo. The first floor porch serves for dining on sunny summer days.

HUDSON HOUSE, 2 Main Street, Cold Spring, NY 10516; (914) 265-9355; Mary Pat Sawyer, Innkeeper. Rates: *moderate*, including continental breakfast. Open all year except month of January; 14 rooms with private baths. Restaurant serves 3 meals daily and Sunday brunch to guests and public; liquor served. Children welcome; Visa, MasterCard, American Express accepted. Sailing yacht, swimming, windsurfing, antiquing, Boscobel, Culinary Institute.

DIRECTIONS: take Rte. 9D to Cold Spring. Just before railroad tracks, bear left and drive over Main Street overpass to the continuation of Main Street. Inn is at end of street on corner. Can also take Metro North from Grand Central Station to Cold Spring station 1 block from inn.

HUNTTING INN

East Hampton   **NEW YORK**

Famous for its restaurant—*The Palm*

At the edge of East Hampton's fashionable shopping district sits The Huntting Inn. Built by Reverend Nathaniel Huntting in 1699, the inn has served as a hostelry since 1751. Although there are few reminders of the days during the American Revolution when the inn was the only neutral meeting spot for the Colonials and Tories, the inn is as popular today as ever, welcoming both overnight guests and diners to its restaurant, The Palm.

The inn is more reminiscent of an old-fashioned, rambling beach cottage than a refined and elegant hostelry, and its mood is appropriately casual and invigorating. Innkeeper Linda Calder has created a warm, lovely décor in the guest rooms, covering the walls with patterned fabric and liberally sprinkling antiques among the furnishings. Accommodations come in many shapes and sizes, from the ample Room 100, which easily houses two antique brass beds, a writing desk, and a Victorian settee and coffee table, to Room 209, a diminutive nest done in shades of jade and peach.

A brick walkway leads from a white picket fence to the inn's front door. In the side yard of the white clapboard, L-shaped cottage, the inn's impressive perennials garden beckons. Throughout the temperate months this bed is a riot of color and fragrance.

A visit to the inn would be incomplete without enjoying a sumptuous, but simple dinner at The Palm.

The inn and restaurant seen from Main Street.

The original restaurant, founded in New York City by Pio Bozzi and John Ganzi in the 1920s, is now operated by their grandsons. It is one of the most popular restaurants in the Hamptons, famous for succulent prime steaks, sweet giant lobsters, and huge portions, served by professional, no-nonsense waiters who bustle about efficiently amidst the jolly atmosphere. The restaurant is simply decorated with pressed-tin ceiling and walls, tongue-in-groove wainscoting, wooden booths, and framed caricatures of the founders and their many famous patrons.

During the summer season, guests enjoy a lavish continental breakfast each morning, featuring an array of fresh fruits, granola, and a large assortment of breads, bagels, and pastries. Off-season guests are treated to a grand selection of turnovers, croissants, muffins, and doughnuts served with yogurt, juice, and hard boiled eggs.

Above, turn-of-the-century bar with its gleaming centerpiece. *Left, top,* The Palm restaurant is renowned for its succulent prime steaks and giant, sweet lobsters. *Bottom,* Room 203 is vibrantly, yet delicately colored.

THE HUNTTING INN, 94 Main Street, East Hampton, Long Island, NY 11937; (516) 324-0410; Linda Calder, Innkeeper. Rates: *moderate* and *expensive*, including continental breakfast. Open April 1 to January 1; 20 rooms with private baths. Included as part of inn is THE PALM restaurant, serving dinner daily from mid-May to mid-September to guests and public; liquor served; live entertainment 5 nights a week during July and August. Children not encouraged; no pets; Spanish spoken; all major credit cards accepted. Golf, deepsea fishing, tennis, riding, antiquing, passes provided in summer for ocean beach ¾ mile from inn.

DIRECTIONS: take Long Island Expressway to exit 70 and drive south to Rte. 27E (Montauk Hwy), which becomes Main Street in East Hampton. Long Island Railroad from Penn Station stops 2 blocks from inn. Hampton Jitney from Manhattan stops at door (details from inn).

THE MILL-GARTH

A beach-oriented country inn

Carriage House, one of several cottages on the property.

The hamlet of Amagansett is a pre-Revolutionary settlement at the tip of Long Island's South Shore. With its proximity to beautiful beaches and relaxed atmosphere geared to the ocean's ebb and flow, Amagansett is a popular escape from the pressures of daily life. A five-minute walk from the center of the village on a shady side street, The Mill-Garth is in perfect sync with the carefree mood of its surroundings. It is a congenial, private, and captivating beach-oriented country inn.

Approaching The Mill-Garth, visitors first notice an antique windmill that marks the edge of the property. This weathered relic recalls the century past—days when miller Abraham Parson lived with his wife, Ellen, on this piece of land and plied his trade. The large, yellow shingle farmhouse at the center of the property was the family homestead, where the Parsons raised their seven children. When Abraham died at the turn of the century, Ellen opened her home to boarders. Since then the inn has gained repute as a special getaway whose atmosphere is relaxing and somewhat addictive.

Innkeepers Burton and Wendy Van Deusen carry on the comfortable tradition of The Mill-Garth. Guests may choose among a wide-ranging array of accommodations, from studio apartments to two-bedroom, two-bath hideaways with living rooms and kitchens. Most rooms are located in the old farmhouse, many with their own private entrances onto a weathered deck, and all with a fully equipped kitchen to free vacationers from planning their lives around restaurant schedules. Several rooms bear the casually sedate look of a traditional country inn while others are simple beach cottages that reflect their windswept and carefree environs. Tucked behind privet hedges and towering shade trees are independent cottages, like the Dairy Cottage, with its old-fashioned kitchen and skylit living room, the more formal Carriage House cloaked in weathered Cape Cod shingles, and the very private, rustic Gazebo.

Above, A second-floor guest room. *Left,* the Dairy Cottage is the quintessential beach cottage—simple and carefree.

THE MILL-GARTH, Windmill Lane, Amagansett, Long Island, NY 11930; (516) 267-3757; Burton and Wendy Van Deusen, innkeepers. Rates: *moderate* and *expensive* (weekly rates only during July and August). Open all year; 12 rooms with private baths and full kitchens. No meals or liquor served; bring your own for use in your own kitchen, or partake of gourmet cuisine 3 miles away at Wendy's parents' inn, the famous 1770 House in East Hampton. Children welcome; well-behaved pets only; no credit cards. Summer theater, golf, tennis, riding, swimming at ocean beach.

DIRECTIONS: take Rte. 27 (Montauk Hwy) to Windmill Lane in Amagansett and turn left to inn. Long Island Railroad from Penn Station; Hampton Jitney from Manhattan (details from inn).

1770 HOUSE

East Hampton   **NEW YORK**

Cordon bleu dishes and antique treasures

The traditional, white-shingled 1770 House nestles unobtrusively under a canopy of greenery along East Hampton's Main Street. Only a small sign announces its identity but word of mouth brings numerous visitors, most of whom come to sample innkeeper Miriam Perle's delicious dinners. A Cordon Bleu alumna with years of experience teaching her own cooking classes, Mim artfully combines a variety of culinary styles to express her own satisfying trademark. Her litany of dishes is long but a random sampling includes appetizers of sliced filet mignon and Chinese vegetables in a ginger vinaigrette as well as rendered pancetta, eggs, and parmesan atop al dente pasta. Entrées such as scallopine of pork in a fresh peach cumberland sauce, a savory boned-and-stuffed capon, and fresh swordfish bathed in a creamy, Greek garlic sauce are likewise accomplished with a deft hand.

The Philip Taylor House.

Above, Wisteria is the largest and most formal guest room in the Philip Taylor House. *Left*, the dark and intimate Taproom, with elegant shell corner case and jewel-like stained glass.

Miriam and husband Sidney are antique-hounds, whose treasures fill the inn. Most striking is the Perles' vast collection of fine clocks, on display in the dining room and library/bar, which include an Act of Parliament clock, a Long Island Railroad regulator—one of four in existence—and an exquisite English grandfather, which presides over the staircase landing. In the dining room the rich rose hue of the décor combines with attractive Regency dining chairs and floral bouquets in antique shaving mugs to set a warm and pleasing tone. Guest bedrooms are furnished with vintage beds, chests, and chairs, which compliment the irregular charm of this antique cottage. Room 10 is a large and particularly pleasant suite with a private entrance, a working fireplace, and a heavily carved bedstead tucked into a draped alcove. Another comfortable favorite is Room 2 on the second floor, where, in winter, guests relax in a canopied bed and gaze into the flickering flames of the open hearth.

A few doors away from the inn proper is the Perles' private residence, a grand Elizabethan manor known as the Philip Taylor House. In one wing three luxurious bedchambers are available to inn guests. The lucky few who enjoy the pleasures of this extraordinary house will find another treat on its grounds, a formal sunken boxwood garden, designed by the first French landscape architect licensed in America. Named after garden flora, the rooms in the house are as different from one another as their namesakes. Pear Tree, for example, offers guests a rustic abode with open beamwork, while Wisteria, in the house's turn-of-the-century addition, delights with gilt and brocade.

1770 HOUSE, 143 Main Street, East Hampton, Long Island, NY 11937; (516) 324-1770; Sidney and Miriam Perle and family, Innkeepers. Rates: 1770 House, *moderate* (off-season) and *expensive*, including breakfast; Philip Taylor House, *expensive*. Open all year; 10 rooms in both houses, with private baths. Dinner served to guests and public at 1770 House, Thursday through Sunday in season, and Friday, Saturday, and all holidays, except Christmas, during off season; liquor served. Children 12 and over welcome; no pets; all major credit cards accepted. Summer theater, antiquing, and other East Hampton activities.

DIRECTIONS: Rte. 27 (Montauk Hwy) to East Hampton. Inn is just beyond village green on left, past cupola-topped Clinton Museum.

Below, Room 12 in 1770 House has its own private entrance from the back garden. *Right*, breakfast under the Perle's prize Act of Parliament clock.

NEW JERSEY

MAINSTAY INN

Perpetual Victorian elegance

Age becomes The Mainstay Inn. Thanks to the unflagging devotion of innkeepers Tom and Sue Carroll, this dowager duchess of Cape May is one of the flagship inns of the East. Guests cannot help but feel pleased and uplifted to be a part of such beauty and elegance.

Left, The Mainstay's Drawing Room recreates an opulent age long past. *Below*, the James Cardinal Gibbons Room is elegant and tranquil.

The inn is situated on a prominent corner two blocks from the ocean, but is shielded by a stand of statuesque sycamores and a fresh white picket fence. The building itself is a perfectly proportioned, symmetrical Victorian mansion painted the color of butterscotch, trimmed with forest green shutters, and supported by slender, beautifully wrought white columns that encircle a broad, wraparound veranda. The top of the mansion is capped by a belvedere that commands a panoramic view of Cape May and its remarkable array of gingerbread castles-by-the-sea. The brick walkway that leads to the Main House also guides guests to the central garden and on to The Mainstay's companion accommodation, which is a separate house called The Cottage. The two houses are like sisters, each with its own beguiling personality. Built by the same architect within two years of one another—1870 and 1872—they blend and complement to create a spacious private compound.

With each passing year the Main House cleaves closer to its elegant character. In the entry hall one's

eye is immediately drawn from thick Oriental rugs which dress gleaming floorboards, past a massive pier glass, up to the ceiling which is bejeweled with intricately patterned paper in regal hues of copper, teal, and cream. The adjoining drawing room reflects an opulent age past, furnished with Victorian chairs and settees in shades of peach, rose, and blue, a baby grand piano, sculpted brocade window dressings, and an assortment of lovely bric-à-brac. Upstairs, each guest room reflects an elegance and softness that suits this grand house.

The Cottage is decorated in a lighter mood as befits its sweet and charming personality. The first floor parlor, with fresh green and pink floral wallpaper, is filled with white wicker furniture accented with deep pink cushions. Guest chambers in this house, which is complemented by a double decker veranda, come in a variety of shapes and sizes, some with living rooms, others with spectacular antique furnishings. Throughout, all is impeccably clean, extremely pleasing, and comfortable.

THE MAINSTAY INN, 635 Columbia Avenue, Cape May, NJ 08204; (609) 884-8690; Tom and Sue Carroll, Innkeepers. Rates: *moderate*, including full breakfast and afternoon tea. Open April through November; 13 rooms (7 in Mainstay, 6 in Cottage), 9 with private baths, 4 sharing 2 baths. Dinner not served; no liquor served (bring your own). Children over 12 welcome; no pets; smoking on veranda only, none indoors; no credit cards accepted. Croquet, swimming at the seashore; bird watching, riding.

DIRECTIONS: the inn is located in the center of town, 2 blocks from Convention Hall.

Above, the main inn building, looking from the porch of the Cottage. *Below*, a sumptuous guest room in the Cottage, with William Morris wallpaper in all its glory. *Opposite page*, the entry hall of the main house reflects the attention to detail for which The Mainstay is noted.

A gingerbread cottage by the sea

In the summer of 1766, Cape May farmer Robert Parsons placed an advertisement in the Pennsylvania Gazette in which he promoted the healthful benefits of bathing in the local waters and offered to open his home to paying guests. Thus began Cape May's guest house trade which, by the mid-1800s had transformed the village into a "watering hole" for the very fashionable, who built gingerbread cottages by the seaside. No single cottage stands out more prominently than The Abbey, owned by innkeepers Jay and Marianne Schatz.

When wealthy coal baron and politician John B. McCreary built The Abbey in 1869 he spared no expense. Given a free hand, the architect created a stunning gothic masterpiece complete with a sixty-foot tower, etched ruby glass, and a fenced widow's walk. So architecturally significant is the building that the Library of Congress holds a set of its measured drawings.

The main parlor, a music room, is a symphony of color and elegance with its formal window dressings, lush gold and ruby wallpaper, gilt moldings, and a ceiling covered with stylized flowers and geometric patterns in blue and burgundy. The adjoining library reveals a muted gold, olive, and brown décor that balances well with two massive glass-fronted cases

The main parlor serves as a music room, with antique harp and 1850 square piano.

filled with antique books, military toys, firearms, and enamel buttons.

Perhaps the most interesting characteristic of The Abbey is that amidst all this grandeur and glory reigns an irrepressibly upbeat and vivacious mood. The Schatzes know how to help people relax and have fun, and because of this rare talent the inn has gained a dedicated following.

Above, an opulently decorative ceiling rosette. *Left*, The Abbey's arresting architecture attracts many admirers.

THE ABBEY, Columbia Avenue and Gurney Street, Cape May, NJ 08204; (609) 884-4506; Jay and Marianne Schatz, Innkeepers. Rates: *moderate*, including full breakfast in spring and fall; lighter buffet in summer; afternoon refreshments. Open April through November; 7 rooms, 4 with private baths and 3 sharing 1 huge bath. Dinner not served; no liquor served (bring your own). Well-behaved children over 12 welcome; no pets; all smoking limited to the veranda; Visa, MasterCard, American Express accepted. Croquet, seashore swimming 1 block from inn, many other activities.

DIRECTIONS: in Cape May, turn left on Ocean Street, drive 3 blocks and turn left on Columbia Avenue. Drive 1 block to inn.

COLLIGAN'S STOCKTON INN

Stockton

NEW JERSEY

"There's a small hotel with a wishing well"

The layers of history at Colligan's Stockton Inn are palpable. First constructed in 1710 when Reading's Ferry attracted settlers to New Jersey's river banks, the building was soon converted into an inn and tavern bearing witness to the Revolution and the birth of a nation. By the twentieth century the property came into the hands of Elizabeth Weiss Colligan who, with her five sons, ran a popular hostelry. The inn was made famous by band leader Paul Whiteman, who frequently broadcast his radio program from the establishment and who dubbed Elizabeth "Ma Colligan." Also musical-comedy song writer Lorenz Hart was inspired to write "There's A Small Hotel" after enjoying a stopover at the inn. Today, this venerable institution is being given a new life under the guidance of veteran innkeepers Todd and Penny Drucquer.

Colligan's sprawling restaurant is located in the original eighteenth-century structure and includes four interior dining rooms, a spacious outdoor patio restaurant complete with waterfall and fish pond, and an old-fashioned tavern. Several of the dining rooms are painted with jewel-like murals which date back to the 1930s when several local artists exchanged painting skills for food and drink. Today's menu offers a far more sophisticated selection than in the past. The chef features a kaleidoscope of seasonal specialties. Constants include baked brie with fresh fruit, mushrooms and artichokes dressed with rasp-

Colligan's is experiencing a renascence, with each guest room restored and beautifully furnished.

berry vinaigrette, veal sautéed with morels and napped with a reduced cream sauce, and boneless roast duckling with brown sugar, Dijon mustard, and black currant sauce. Because Todd loves wine and hopes his guests will share in this pleasure, he adds just five dollars to his cost which makes for wonderful times at a great bargain.

Over the past several years the Drucquers renovated all of the guest rooms, which are located upstairs and in the three separate buildings. Two of the largest suites in the inn proper open onto the second story veranda that overlooks the village of Stockton. The Wagon House and the Carriage House adjoin the inn and house classic and comfortable chambers. Across the street is a beautifully refurbished Federal-style house that contains rooms, suites, and a garden apartment that opens onto a private brick patio. Each and every room throughout the inn is freshly fitted with lovely draperies, linens, and rugs in an appealing blend of lush colors and rich textures.

COLLIGAN'S STOCKTON INN, Rte. 29, Stockton, NJ 08559; (609) 397-1250 or (800) 368-7272; Todd Drucquer, Innkeeper. Rates: *moderate*, including continental breakfast. Open all year; 7 suites and 4 rooms, many with fireplaces, all with private baths. Restaurant serves 2 meals daily and special Sunday brunch to guests and public; 3 bars serve light bar menu. Children over 8 welcome; no pets; all major credit cards accepted. Dancing some evenings at inn, Bucks County activities nearby.

DIRECTIONS: Stockton is on Rte. 29 on the east side of the Delaware River from Bucks County.

PENNSYLVANIA

INN AT STARLIGHT LAKE

Starlight   **PENNSYLVANIA**

The last railroad guest house in existence

The foothills of the Moosic Mountains run along the western edge of the Catskills, and the terrain rolls and climbs, creating niches that hide glacial lakes and private valleys. It is in one of these small valleys that The Inn at Starlight Lake is tucked away. The inn sprawls along the placid lakefront looking much as it has since the early 1900s, when it was a summer guest house serving passengers on the Ontario and Western Railroad. Today the inn is the last railroad guest house in existence and as such has been recognized by the National Register of Historic Places.

This is a wonderfully relaxing environment, having changed little in the eighty-odd years of its existence. Innkeepers Judy and Jack McMahon have added all the conveniences necessary to the contemporary traveler while carefully maintaining the pervading spirit of unselfconscious sweetness. The large lobby sets the overall mood for the entire inn, and guests know at a glance that they've arrived at an authentic, old-time country inn. One corner of the lobby is given over to reading and relaxing; its focal point, surrounded by inviting easy chairs, is a hewn-stone fireplace with a collection of cocks, pheasants, and mallards displayed on its mantel. In another corner

sits a baby grand piano loaded with sheet music and lit by a floor lamp whose stained-glass shade is decorated with a musical staff and clef. The McMahons left careers in the legitimate theater for the intimate theater of an inn, and this corner is a reminder of their abiding interest in music and entertainment.

The inn offers as many pastimes as larger resorts without succumbing to impersonal regimentation. Tennis, swimming, boating, fishing, lawn games, bicycling, and cross-country skiing can all be enjoyed on the premises. Sharpened appetites are cared for in the dining room, a large sun porch that looks out toward the lake. Generous portions of such dishes as veal française, sirloin steak au poivre, flaming roast duckling, pork chops with mustard pickle sauce, and the house favorite, Jaeger Schnitzel, leave little room for dessert, but when faced with these homemade sweets, resistance melts. The inn's gifted baker also prepares moist and fragrant loaves of bread each day.

Guest rooms are located on the two top floors of the inn and in several cottages. Furnishings throughout are a mixture of antiques and comfortable pieces that make for an easy, old-fashioned air.

Above, guest rooms are simple and unpretentious, but individually decorated. *Left, top*, fishing in the early morning mist. *Bottom*, misty view of the inn from the dock. *Previous pages*, The Inn at Starlight Lake.

THE INN AT STARLIGHT LAKE, Starlight, PA 18461; (717) 798-2519; Judy and Jakc McMahon, Innkeepers. Rates: *moderate*, including breakfast and dinner. Open all year, except April 1 to 15; 27 rooms, most with private baths. Restaurant serves 3 meals daily to guests and public; liquor served. No pets; Visa and MasterCard accepted. Fishing in trophy waters for trout and smallmouth bass, swimming, boating, tennis, cycling, hiking, antiquing.

DIRECTIONS: from I-81 take exit 62 to Rte. 107 east into Rte. 247 to Forest City. Turn left on Rte. 171.

Milford # CLIFF PARK INN **PENNSYLVANIA**

Where good food and golf are among life's essentials

The care and concern lavished on Cliff Park Inn is apparent from the moment one arrives. This charming, old edifice is an American treasure that was built as a farmhouse in 1820 by George Buchanan. Generations of Buchanans have since cherished this stunning homestead high atop the palisades at the headwaters of the Delaware River. A long, open porch runs the entire length of the large, white-frame structure. Green wicker rockers and armchairs line this porch and offer the perfect spot for observing golfers plying their skill on the inn's beautifully landscaped, nine-hole course which, before being converted in 1913, was once rolling farmlands. Inn guests enjoy beautifully maintained greens, a top-

Left, the inn and golf course, in the gently rolling Pennsylvania countryside. *Below*, the original farmhouse has grown over the years into a rambling white clapboard inn.

notch pro shop, and the services of the Cliff Park golf pro. Yet non-golfers need not fear being overwhelmed. Rather, this gentle sport adds an interesting dimension to the inn's multilayered personality. Those who enjoy being surrounded by lovely antiques will find themselves in heaven here. Family heirlooms are found in every nook and cranny, and one of the most inviting rooms, the large parlor, is filled with ancestral portraits and pieces collected by Buchanans over the years. A visit to the dining room recalls Sunday at grandma's house, with heavy tables draped in lace, sideboards laden with antique glassware, and plate rails lined with assorted bric-à-brac.

The Buchanan family believes good food is among life's essentials, and for this reason they make dining at Cliff Park a satisfying treat. The dinner menu offers wide and interesting choices, from terrine of lemon sole wrapped in spinach, and salade niçoise, to stuffed quail napped with truffle sauce, and tournedos of beef glistening with brandy glacé and served with pâté, artichokes, and mushrooms. The kitchen also offers a no-butter, no-salt entrée, which reflects what is freshest in the market.

After dinner, guests might sit before the fire, play cards, read, or retire to their rooms, located on the

upper floors of the main inn or in three separate cottages, the Club Cottage, Garden Cottage, and Augusta House. With exposed beams and a large fieldstone fireplace, the Club Cottage is especially attractive and is furnished with a collection of pieces dating to the mid-1950s, that were assembled by an aunt who called the cottage "home."

CLIFF PARK INN, Milford, PA 18337; (717) 296-6491; The Buchanan Family, Innkeepers. Rates: *moderate*, including breakfast, lunch, and dinner. Open Memorial Day to end of October; 10 rooms in inn, 7 rooms in 2 cottages, plus 5-room cottage, all with private baths. Dining room serves 3 meals daily to guests and public; liquor served. Children welcome; horse stables available for boarding; major credit cards accepted. 9 hole golf course, 7 miles of hiking trails, good antiquing and tennis nearby.

DIRECTIONS: take I-80 to Rte. 15 into Rte. 206 to Milford. Inn is located 1½ miles northwest of Milford. Watch for signs for inn. Short Line bus from New York Port Authority, pickup available. Scranton/Wilkes Barre airport for scheduled flights.

Opposite page, the Club Cottage, with its art deco screen door, *top*, and one of its idiosyncratic bedrooms as decorated by a beloved aunt. *Below*, guests enjoy kibbitzing the golfers from the comfortable porch. *Right*, Harry Buchanan, head of the clan, in full dress.

Canadensis # OVERLOOK INN **PENNSYLVANIA**

Born innkeepers instill an atmosphere of good cheer

The porch at The Overlook Inn feels like a tree house for grown-ups. This second-story retreat, filled with glistening white wicker furniture and brightly colored cushions, offers a view of the treetops and a concert of birdsong. Amidst this abundant greenery, it is difficult to imagine that, not long ago, the surrounding acres were farmland and the inn a rambling farmhouse.

In 1910, the Thomases, who owned the then farm, invited their relatives to visit their cool mountain retreat for the season. After a summer of feeding the hungry hordes, Mrs. Thomas wisely decided to turn her efforts into a profitable occupation and, starting with family, opened a boarding house. A decade later, burgeoning automobile and train travelers created the Pocono tourist industry, and the Thomases' boarding house grew into a hotel.

The inn today is an old-fashioned classic, its main living room and game room filled with a comfortable assortment of lovely antiques and traditional furnishings. Everything here tells the visitor, "Relax, you've come home." To add to the atmosphere of good cheer, owners Bob and Lolly Tupper are born innkeepers, greeting each and every guest with warmth and interest, and instilling The Overlook with an easy, unpretentious spirit. Lolly decorated most of

Pierre's breakfast popovers.

the bedrooms, which reflect that same feeling of casual comfort.

The Overlook's dining room attracts a large following from the surrounding populace, most of whom dress in their best bib and tucker and often arrive early for a before-theater repast. Homemade soups and breads accompany a good selection of tempting entrées, including house specials like chicken ambrosiana; quail stuffed with a mélange of rices; filet of beef in a sour cream–cognac–mushroom sauce; and Pennsylvania brook trout. Overnight guests are treated to a yeoman's breakfast, a meal large enough to set them up for the day. The selection may include banana pecan pancakes, a ham, swiss, and tomato omelet; French toast; fresh-squeezed orange juice or fresh fruit; scrapple, ham, or bacon; Lolly's especially fine homemade jam; and the *pièce de résistance,* Pierre's popovers, which are crusty on the outside, slightly creamy on the inside, and capped with toasted almonds.

Above, Lolly's bedrooms have a homey, old fashioned air. *Left,* the treetop porch, *top,* and a view of the inn from the pool, *bottom.*

THE OVERLOOK INN, Dutch Hill Road, Canadensis, PA 18325; (717) 595-7519; Bob and Lolly Tupper, Innkeepers. Rates: *moderate,* including country breakfast and full dinner. Open all year; 20 rooms, including 2 suites (12 in main house, 6 in lodge, and 2 in carriage house), all with private baths. Dining room serves breakfast and dinner daily to guests and public (by reservation). Special New Year's Day brunch; bar serving liquor. Children over 12 welcome; no pets; Spanish and French spoken; major credit cards accepted. Swimming pool, shuffleboard, bocci, library. Golf, tennis, downhill and cross-country skiing, and antiquing nearby.

DIRECTIONS: From I-80 drive west to exit 52 and follow Rte. 447 north through Canadensis to 1st traffic light; ½ mile past light, turn right onto Dutch Hill Road to inn.

PINE KNOB INN

Canadensis **PENNSYLVANIA**

An impressive complex, including an art gallery and workshops

The Pine Knob is a spacious inn with a feeling of intimacy. Its impressive complex comprises a large board-and-battan, Victorian "cottage," three out-cottages, and an art gallery/workshop in the converted barn, all surrounded by gardens, shrubbery, and towering old trees. Across the road, there are the inn's swimming pool, gazebo, and gate to picturesque Brodhead Creek. The feeling of intimacy that ties all this together originates with innkeepers June and Jim Belfie, whose genuine warmth and easy smiles fill the inn with hospitality.

The main house was built by Dr. Gilbert Palen in the mid-1800s, during the time when his tannery business, the mainstay of the local economy, was thriving. Palen renamed the town Canadensis after the hemlock tree on which the tanning business depended. Unfortunately, by the 1870s the supply of hemlock grew sparse, business waned, and, eventually Palen's house was converted into a fashionable mountain guest retreat.

The dining room at the Pine Knob is among the best in the area. The inn's dedicated and talented chef is happiest when creating new and delicious ways to prepare food, and standouts include home-made wholewheat pasta served with rounds of delicate veal sausage, scallops stuffed with salmon paste, and a Cornish game hen glazed with a tangy straw-berry vinaigrette sauce. Fresh breads, soups, and desserts are prepared daily as well.

In between repasts, guests enjoy rocking on the inn's front porch or relaxing in the main parlor, which easily accommodates June's grand piano, a mix of comfortable antiques, and an every-changing gallery of paintings, sculpture, and photographs. June is avidly interested in the arts and, since innkeepers can't get away to attend workshops, has decided to bring workshops to the inn. The roster of gifted artists who hold classes here grows in quality, quantity, and renown with each passing year.

This area is the prettiest part of the Poconos, retaining its quiet, natural beauty. Guests at the Pine Knob enjoy simple pleasures, picnicking on the flat, smooth rocks of the Brodhead Creek, reading in the large, comfortable parlor, or retreating to an old-fashioned bedroom for a nap. June decorates guest rooms with antiques and favors colors that feel restful and inviting.

Above, each guest room is furnished with a pleasing mixture of antiques and old-fashioned pieces, all in quiet and restful hues. *Left*, always a useful adjunct to an inn.

PINE KNOB INN, Rte. 447, Canadensis, PA 18325; (717) 595-2532; June and Jim Belfie, Innkeepers. Rates: *inexpensive*, with full breakfast and gourmet dinner included. Closed during December; 27 rooms, including 18 in main house, 4 each in 2 cottages, and 1 in bungalow; most rooms with private baths, some share. Dining room open 7 days a week for 2 meals, for guests and the public by reservation. Candlelight dining with classical background music. Bar serves liquor. Non-smoking dining room available; children 5 and up welcome; no pets; Visa and MasterCard accepted. Swimming pool, tennis court, hiking, trout stream on premises. Antiquing, summer theater, golfing, cross-country skiing, boating, horseback riding. DIRECTIONS: from I-80, near Stroudsburg on Pennsylvania side of Delaware River, take exit 52 onto Rte. 447 north towards Canadensis. Watch for inn sign before Canadensis.

Bloomsburg INN AT TURKEY HILL **PENNSYLVANIA**

A beautifully conceived inn

Travelers on Interstate 80 might raise a skeptical eyebrow at the thought of an oasis of charm and comfort materializing beside such a roadway. But Babs Eyerly Pruden, owner and innkeeper of The Inn at Turkey Hill, offers wayfarers along this broad ribbon of highway just that.

The solid and elegant white brick farmhouse that houses the inn's restaurant was the Eyerly homestead until Babs and her journalist/gentleman farmer father decided Bloomsburg needed a first-class inn. Though her father died before the project was completed Babs carried on with the dream. The result is an immaculate and beautifully designed complex; a meandering semicircle of white clapboard guest rooms, each with a view toward the duckpond which sits at the center of the inn complex. Guests are transported to a tranquil world as ducks glide across the pond and graceful ferns and Japanese iris cluster around the base of the lacy gazebo.

Back at the main house three meals a day are served each day of the year. In the Mural Room, one of the two formal dining rooms, there are rich handpainted scenes of Pennsylvania's rolling countryside on the walls, and the tables are draped in pink damask and decorated with potted African violets. Another favorite is the Greenhouse dining room that overlooks the duck pond and gazebo. Striped canvas at the ceiling, which shields diners

Handpainted mural in one of the two formal dining rooms.

from the midday sun, rolls back to reveal the stars at night. The dinner menu offers a well-balanced range of dishes: clams or oysters dressed with spinach, sour cream, horseradish, cheese, and bacon; homemade soups; capellini with spicy fennel sausage in cream sauce; rabbit marinated in burgundy and sautéed with fresh herbs; duck stuffed with wild rice, walnuts, and raisins and bathed in a tangy lingonberry sauce.

As beautiful as Turkey Hill is, it wouldn't be half as charming without Babs's enthusiasm and devotion. Her greatest desire is for each of her guests to feel special, and she has imbued her staff with an attitude of caring.

Above, guest rooms are furnished with handmade reproductions from Georgia's Habersham Plantation. *Left, top*, entrance to the inn. *Bottom*, handpainted decorations in the other formal dining room.

THE INN AT TURKEY HILL, 911 Central Road, Bloomsburg, PA 17815; (717) 387-1500; Babs Pruden, Innkeeper. Rates: *moderate*, including continental breakfast. Open all year, 19 rooms, including 2 suites with fireplaces and double Jacuzzis, all with private baths. Restaurant serves 3 meals daily, with special Sunday brunch, to guests and public; no cigar or pipe smoking in dining rooms; liquor served. Children welcome; all major credit cards accepted. TV in rooms; antiquing, golf, fishing, hunting, boating, covered bridges nearby.

DIRECTIONS: the inn is at exit 35 on I-80 on the corner at first red light. Wilkes-Barre/Scranton nearest airport; arrange for pickup.

Steeped in America's past

At the Century Inn history is palpable. The original hewn-stone building was constructed as an inn in 1794 by the Hill family, founders of the village of Scenery Hill.

With a thoughtful blend of antique and traditional furnishings, Century Inn strikes an easy balance between museum and home and resonates years of tender, loving care. From the moment the guests enter, they are steeped in America's past. Two front parlors contain lusterware, antique paperweights, and colored glassware, but most prized by innkeepers Megin and Gordon Harrington is their display of Gallatin glass and an original flag from the Whiskey Rebellion, which hangs above the hearth. What is now the inn's tavern was originally the innkeeper's bedroom, and since this chamber was cut off from traffic, it has retained its original floorboards and woodwork, all in mint condition. Among the antiques-filled, upstairs guest rooms is one named for Dolly Madison, which houses a large collection of antique dolls, toys, miniature furniture, china, and an illuminated dollhouse.

Century Inn is a popular dining spot and its most sought-after tables are found in the Keeping Room, which served as the original kitchen. Antique kitchen

Part of the famous doll collection.

utensils, a hand-forged crane, and a large collection of salt-glazed crockery are displayed around the large cooking hearth. At the rear of the building is another favorite dining room with banks of windows looking out to the sweeping back lawn. The inn's bill of fare features straightforward American cooking, from roast turkey and stuffed pork chops to broiled seafoods and steaks. The luncheon menu offers a varied selection which includes Welsh rarebit with bacon, tomato, and cole slaw; baked brie with almonds and fresh fruit; and an array of sandwiches, salads, and hot entrées.

The inn is the dominant presence in this diminutive town, which can be explored in an easy evening constitutional. Along the way visitors pass a beautifully restored residence that houses the Harringtons' gift shop, named Forever Christmas. Here, Megin's favorite holiday is richly represented in room after room of cheering and beautifully wrought yuletide treasures.

Above, the David Bradford Room, with fishnet canopied bed and portraits of George and Martha Washington framed above the headboard. *Left*, lovely landscaping and colorful gardens accent the hewn stone of the Century Inn. *Overleaf*, the Keeping Room hearth in the dining room, one of the favorite rooms in the inn.

CENTURY INN, Main Street, Scenery Hill, PA 15360; (412) 945-6600 or 5180; Megin and Gordon Harrington, Innkeepers. Rates: *moderate*. Closed mid-December to mid-March; 6 rooms with private baths. Dining room serves 3 meals daily, breakfast to guests only and lunch and dinner to public; liquor served. Children welcome; no pets; credit cards not accepted. Antiquing, horse racing, white-water rafting, Frank Lloyd Wright house nearby. Pittsburgh 35 miles away.

DIRECTIONS: from east, leave Pennsylvania Turnpike at New Stanton and take I-70 west to Rte. 917 south (Bentleyville exit), to Rte. 40E and go 1 mile to inn. From west, take I-70 east to I-79 south, to Rte. 40E, 9 miles to inn.

Ephrata # SMITHTON **PENNSYLVANIA**

Legendary Pennsylvania Dutch hospitality

The town of Ephrata is a perfect starting place for exploring colorful Lancaster County, and Smithton is the most charming and comfortable hostelry from which to base the adventure. The inn is an historic stone house which was built in 1762 by Henry and Susana Miller, who were "outdoor members" of the Ephrata Community, a Protestant monastic sect under the charismatic leadership of Johann Conrad Beissel. His community practiced celibacy and asceticism, and they built an elegant cluster of medieval German buildings, called the Cloister, by the banks of Cocalico Creek. Meanwhile the Millers opened a tavern and inn that, according to one traveler's diary, "was a good and proper house that would not offend a lady."

Pennsylvania Dutch hospitality is legendary, and Smithton's innkeeper Dorothy Graybill is a true native who sees to it that her guests are well-cared for. Her first point of order is to make certain each simple and comfortable guest room is laden with thoughtful amenities. To this end she hangs soft flannel nightshirts, color coordinated to the scheme of the room, on plain wooden pegs behind bedroom doors. Color plays an important part in these chambers, and the focal point of each is a handmade Pennsylvania Dutch

quilt of such vibrancy and liveliness it is apparent why they are sought after by collectors of American crafts. On top of the quilts are oversized down pillows, edged with ruffles, perfect for propping up in bed for a good read. Every room has a working fireplace, which adds immeasurably to the overall spirit of cheer and warmth.

In the morning a country breakfast is served in the inn's sunny dining room amidst a whimsical collection of local crafts. Dorothy also makes available a light and satisfying dinner to guests who choose to stay close to the hearth and home, and from time to time she might prepare a gala feast, which weaves an especially festive mood for weekend visitors.

After a good night's sleep guests are ready to discover the character and charms of Lancaster County. The county is a fascinating amalgam, one that neatly combines the ever-fascinating horse-and-buggy culture of Amish and Mennonite "plain people" with the complexities of modern life.

Above, the Blue Room, with velvet canopy. Fluffy, ruffled prop-up pillows add comfort to each bed—one of many thoughtful details. *Left*, colorful handmade Amish quilts brighten each bed. This suite has a plaster mural showing innkeeper Dorothy Graybill and her "pet" groundhog, Hogmalion.

SMITHTON, 900 West Main Street, Ephrata, PA 17522; (717) 733-6094; Dorothy Graybill, Innkeeper. Rates: *inexpensive* to *expensive*, including lavish Pennsylvania Dutch breakfast. Open all year; 5 rooms and 1 suite, all with private baths. Dining room open 7 nights serving dinner to guests only. Supervised children and pets welcome. Visa, MasterCard, American Express accepted. Pennsylvania Dutch Country museums, crafts, and antiques nearby. Smithton tours of Pennsylvania Dutch Country available 6 days at extra charge.

DIRECTIONS: from Pennsylvania Turnpike at exit 21 take Rte. 222 to Ephrata exit. From south take Rte. 222 north to the Ephrata exit. Turn west onto Rte. 322 (Ephrata's Main Street) and drive 2½ miles to inn, which is on the corner of Rte. 322 and Academy Drive.

FAIRFIELD INN

Turning back the pages of time

Fairfield, Pennsylvania is the embodiment of small-town America, a village where visitors feel they've turned back the pages of time and entered a simpler life. In town, the single main street invites a leisurely stroll before rolling up its sidewalks early each evening. A few miles down country roads that wander through scenic orchards and past covered bridges is historic Gettysburg, site of one of the most decisive battles of the Civil War and scene of President Lincoln's famous address.

Returning to Fairfield, visitors find the historic Fairfield Inn in step with the mood of Gettysburg. The beautiful 1757 stone structure with its two-story, open gallery sits directly on the sidewalk of Main Street, a witness to America's founding days. Patrick Henry, J.E.B. Stuart, and Thaddeus Stevens, father of public schools, were guests at the inn, and General Robert E. Lee marched his men past in defeat after the decisive Battle of Gettysburg. On that somber day townsfolk lined the roadway in front of the inn to feed the starving, exhausted soldiers from large, iron cauldrons filled with nourishing bean soup. This same recipe appears on the inn's menu today.

The inn is known for its classic country fare, and its most popular dish is chicken and biscuits, generously dressed with a delicate, translucent gravy. The menu's other staples include country ham, prime rib of beef, crab cakes, and grilled pork chops, all accompanied by feather-light fritters, vegetables served family-style, and hot southern biscuits with lots of butter and honey. Succulent, homemade black raspberry pie draws raves, though one should give serious thought before turning down a mocha pecan ice cream ball with hot fudge sauce, the creamy rice pudding, or another of the flaky-crusted fruit pies made by a gifted, local octogenarian.

Above, the most popular and savory dish at the inn is chicken and biscuits. *Left*, the oldest dining room in the inn is the smallest and most charming, with its uneven floorboards, stone walls, and large hearth with broad mantel.

FAIRFIELD INN, P.O. Box 196, Fairfield, PA 17320; (717) 642-5410; David Thomas, Innkeeper. Rates: *inexpensive*. Open all year, except for major holidays, first week in September, and first week in February; 6 rooms, (2 rooms in inn and 4 rooms in guest house down the street), sharing baths. Restaurant open to guests and public Monday to Saturday: breakfast 8–10 A.M., lunch 11–2 P.M., dinner 5–8:30 P.M. Open for brunch Sundays from April to October, noon–2:30 P.M.; liquor served. No pets; Visa and MasterCard accepted. Gettysburg, Eisenhower farm, golfing, swimming, downhill skiing, Totem Pole Playhouse in summer.

DIRECTIONS: from Gettysburg follow Rte. 116 west 8 miles to Fairfield. Inn is in center of the village. Pickup can be arranged from bus stop in Gettysburg.

JOSEPH AMBLER INN

North Wales   **PENNSYLVANIA**

A handsome fieldstone manor house

When Joseph Ambler obtained 150 acres of land from William Penn in 1734, he built a small but sturdy house in the rolling Pennsylvania countryside. That tiny house laid the cornerstone for what, today, is the Joseph Ambler Inn's impressive fieldstone manor house.

By 1820 Squire John Roberts, a prosperous lawyer, married into the Ambler family and became lord of the manor. He added on to his father-in-law's house in order to accommodate a growing family; he also erected a large and handsome fieldstone barn and a tenant farmer's clapboard cottage. By the twentieth century the Wright family attached a schoolroom to what now had grown into a rambling country house.

In contrast to those days of yore, the Ambler Inn is close to civilization, to downtown Philadelphia, historic Valley Forge, and beautiful Bucks County. But the inn embodies gracious estate living amidst encroaching development. Innkeepers Steve and Terry Kratz infuse the Joseph Ambler with an enthusiasm that enlivens the formal house and its elegant surroundings. Among their many talents, Steve is gaining a reputation for his breakfast spread, especially Ambler Inn French toast made from thick, crusty slices of French bread.

Guests first enter the formal sitting room, which is filled with period furniture, a lovely hearth, and original, random-width pine floorboards. Immediately to one's left is the schoolroom, its lusterous flooring covered with tapestry rugs. A walk-in fireplace, built-in bookshelves, a large writing desk, and an assortment of inviting sofas make this one of the warmest rooms in the house. On the other side of the parlor is Joseph Ambler's original house, which is now the informal sitting room offering a good selection of readable paperback books and board games. Guest rooms are located on either one of the two top floors of the house; in the annex, which is connected by a portico; or in the refurbished tenant farmer's residence, called Corybeck House. Each is furnished with a blend of antiques and good period

Left, the handsome, fieldstone manor house contains a collection of charming and comfortable guest rooms such as the Wright, *bottom*, a romantic nook tucked into the eaves of the third floor.

Breakfast might include the Ambler's savory French toast.

reproductions. Some are formal and cool in mood; others are softly romantic. The Allman Suite, with its own greenhouse sitting room, is a favorite honeymoon retreat.

Midweek, the inn is a popular resting spot for traveling executives who enjoy staying in homelike surroundings. For their comfort each room is equipped with a color television and telephone. Weekend guests enjoy being so near, yet so far, from the pressures of the daily grind.

JOSEPH AMBLER INN, 1005 Horsham Road, North Wales, PA 19454; (215) 362-7500; Steve and Terry Kratz, Managers. Rates: *moderate* and *expensive*, including full breakfast. Open all year; 15 rooms, private baths. No restaurant or bar; bring your own liquor. No children under 12; no pets; French spoken; major credit cards accepted. Valley Forge, New Hope, Philadelphia, antiques shops and restaurants nearby; Mercer Tile in Doylestown.

DIRECTIONS: inn is actualy in Montgomeryville; take Pennsylvania Turnpike to Fort Washington exit. Follow Rte. 309 north to 2nd stoplight. Turn right onto Stump Rd. and then left at first light onto Horsham Rd. (Rte. 463), Inn is approximately 100 yds. on right.

EVERMAY ON-THE-DELAWARE

Erwinna

PENNSYLVANIA

Serene elegance— memorable cuisine

Situated along a shady stretch of River Road, that narrow byway which parallels the Delaware River and its adjoining canal and towpath, Evermay on-the-Delaware is doubly blessed. Though close to the colorful hustle-and-bustle of Bucks County, the inn is separate and serene. To make things perfect, this handsome, nineteenth-century mansion is cared for by superlative, veteran innkeepers Ron Strouse and Fred Cresson.

One enters the inn to discover two elegant adjoining parlors. Corner sofas and conversation groupings before the two fireplaces offer comfort and a perfect vantage point for admiring matched crystal chandeliers, tapestry area rugs, and a one-of-a-kind Victorian "primitive" grandfather clock. Tea is served in these adjoining parlors, and also, before dinner one may enjoy an apèritif while perusing the wide selection of magazines stacked on a softly lit table.

Dinner, a leisurely meal served on Friday, Saturday, Sunday, and major holidays, is an affair to remember. Chef Ron starts guests with a tiny plate of hors d'oeuvres, followed by soup, an appetizer, salad, a choice of three entrées, fruit and cheese plate, dessert, and finally a plate of delicate cookies. The wide-ranging variety of tastes and textures in one meal

Innkeeper Ron Strouse, also the chef.

might include a miniature Maryland crabcake; strawberry soup with Bordeaux, sour cream, and nutmeg; sautéed sweetbreads and chicken served with fresh tomato sauce; noisettes of lamb wrapped in bacon and served with green peppercorn butter; and Fred's celestial macadamia nut brittle ice cream nested on an almond meringue and capped with whipped cream.

After such a repast it is with a sense of deep comfort that one stumbles upstairs to one's room. Guest rooms at Evermay, which include a separate two-story carriage house, are antiques-filled, simple, and comfortable. The Samuel Ingham Room—all rooms are named after a luminary of the past who lived in Bucks County—is especially attractive, its great overstuffed cut-velvet armchair yielding a view of the majestic Delaware.

Above, guest rooms are furnished with Victorian carved beds and period antiques befitting the vintage of the building. *Left*, Evermay stands alone on a large sweep of tree-studded lawn facing the Delaware River.

EVERYMAY ON-THE-DELAWARE, River Road, Erwinna, PA 18920; (215) 294-9100; Ron Strouse and Fred Cresson, Innkeepers. Rates: *moderate*, including continental breakfast. Open all year except for December 24th; 13 rooms, including 3 suites, all with private baths. Dining room open Friday, Saturday, Sunday, and major holidays for dinner, for guests and public; liquor served. No children under 12; no pets; no cigars or pipes in dining room; major credit cards accepted. Bucks County recreation including ballooning, canoeing, antiquing, tubing, golf, swimming.

DIRECTIONS: from New York City take Rte. 22 to Clinton; Rte. 31 to Flemington; Rte. 12 to Frenchtown. Cross Delaware River and drive south on Rte. 32, 2 miles to inn. From Philadelphia take I-95 north to Yardley exit and Rte. 32 north to Erwinna and the inn. West Hunterdon Transit bus service to Frenchtown from New York City. Pickup can be arranged.

New Hope INN AT PHILLIPS MILL **PENNSYLVANIA**

The gem of Bucks County

River Road is a narrow back road that traces the banks of the Delaware River, passing along shaded stretches and through small settlements. Located on a sinuous bend in the road is a charming stone and mortar inn with a chubby copper piglet swinging above the entry. Hanging baskets of flowers and a privacy fence partially obscure the building, but a door painted soft, deep blue marks the entrance. There could be no more romantic setting for a country hideaway than that enjoyed by The Inn at Phillips Mill.

The inn dates back to 1750 when, as a barn, it was part of Aaron Phillips' gristmill. The mill operated until 1900 when landscape painter William Lathrop bought the mill and surrounding acreage and formed Bucks County's first artist's colony. By the early 1970s the property, which by then had the look of an old English village, captured the imagination of Joyce and Brooks Kaufman, and two innkeepers were born. With Joyce's refined sense of color and Brook's accomplished skill as an architect they transformed the space and created five very individual guest rooms, three indoor dining rooms, and a vine-encrusted, walled garden. The atmosphere is pure romance.

The Kaufmans tucked guest rooms into nooks and crannies to create an element of charming discovery. Favorites include Room 2, which is a two-room suite

View of alfresco garden dining area from sunporch dining room. Intimacy is assured with a few tables well spaced for privacy.

with a small sitting room furnished in wicker and cane pieces cushioned in Provençal fabrics. Passing through Dutch doors one enters the bedroom with its iron and brass bed, oil paintings, and floral wallpaper. The color palette Joyce chose for this suite is delicate but rich, blending shades of green, rose, mauve, grape, and cream. At the other end of the spectrum, Room 4 is pure fancy with deep rose walls, imported Indian rugs, a rattan table painted bottle green, and a bed tucked into an alcove and framed by printed draperies.

Phillips Mill has long been known for it kitchen, and the inn's intimate dining rooms set the proper mood to thoroughly enjoy the chef's prowess. The menu is decidedly French and might feature mousse of smoked trout, pear, and salmon with sauce grêlette; a salad of haricot verts and fresh tomatoes in a cream dressing; a salmon napoleon in a pool of watercress sauce; and tournedos of beef served with an artichoke bottom, napped with Bearnaise. The number of dining tables is kept to a minimum in order that the sense of privacy be preserved.

Above, Room 3 is a charming third floor garret. *Left*, Phillips Mill, nestled on a bend in the River Road.

THE INN AT PHILLIPS MILL, North River Road, New Hope, PA 18938; (215) 862-2984; Brooks and Joyce Kaufman, Innkeepers. Rates: *moderate*, with extra charge for continental breakfast. Closed early January through early February; 5 rooms, all with private baths. Restaurant open daily serving dinner to guests and public; bring your own liquor. Children over 6 welcome; no pets; French spoken; no credit cards accepted. Swimming pool on premises; towpath, Bucks County nearby.

DIRECTIONS: Inn is located 1½ miles north of New Hope on River Road (Rte. 32).

BARLEY SHEAF FARM

Holicong **PENNSYLVANIA**

Life went to a party here

Hidden at the end of a long, tree-shaded lane, Barley Sheaf Farm is surrounded by fenced acres dotted with woolly, grazing sheep. Though located in the midst of the hurly burly of the once bucolic Bucks County, it is imbued with a sense of calm, of being a world removed. For years the private home of innkeepers Ann and Don Mills, the inn is filled with the grace notes of a life well-lived. Ann's delicate paintings, family photographs, antique bureaus displaying charming perfume bottles, and the miscellaneous bric-a-brac gathered over a lifetime, allow guests a feeling of instant rapport which, in turn, gives way to instant relaxation. But it is not only the Mills's life that echoes through the inn; shades of the people who have passed through this stone mansion create a special mood.

The oldest section of the house was built in 1740 and grew over the years to encompass a large formal living room, a wood-paneled sitting room, a sun porch-breakfast room, and a generous supply of bedrooms on the second and third floors. Earlier in this century, the house enjoyed an exciting and glamourous period when it was owned by playwright George S. Kaufman. Life magazine captured a memorable photo of Harpo Marx doing a handstand by

The Mansard-roofed inn has been the site of many good times.

the swimming pool when it went to a party at the Kaufman estate. Other luminaries of that day who frequented the Kaufman's home included Lillian Hellman, Alexander Woollcott, S.J. Perlman, and Moss Hart.

Life at Barley Sheaf begins with breakfast on the sun porch which overlooks the lawn, the pool, and the pond beyond. Ann features foods produced right on the farm—honey, raspberries, eggs, and fresh-baked breads. Nectarines and blueberries with brandied cream, French toast stuffed with citrus cheese filling, homemade sausage, country eggs with salsa and sour cream, moist scone bread, pancakes and fresh raspberry sauce capped with nutmeg-flecked sour cream, honey-glazed ham—the parade of delicacies that have trooped from her kitchen seems endless and endlessly delicious.

Above, Room 1 is a spacious suite with an antique brass sleigh bed, French doors opening onto a tiny patio, and handpainted screen—all in shades of celery, cream, and green. *Left*, Room 4 is the perfect country inn bedroom—honest, serene, and very comfortable, with lots of grace notes.

BARLEY SHEAF FARM, Box 10, Route 202, Holicong, PA 18928; (215) 794-5104; Ann and Don Mills, and Don Mills Jr., Innkeepers. Rates: *moderate*, including full breakfast. Open all year except period from December 21 through first weekend in January. Open weekends only from first week in January to mid-February. 9 rooms, 6 in main house and 3 in separate "Ice House" cottage, all with private baths. No restaurant or bar; liquor permitted. Children over 8 welcome; no pets; French spoken; Visa accepted. Swimming pool, croquet, Bucks County, antiques, ballooning, tubing on river, cross-country skiing, towpath.

DIRECTIONS: from New York City take I-95 south to exit 10. Take Rte. 287 north to Rtes. 202/206 heading south (towards Princeton). Follow to circle in Somerville and take Rte. 202 south to Pennsylvania border (about 40 minutes). Continue on Rte. 202 south for 8 minutes to inn on left side of road.

MARYLAND

ROBERT MORRIS INN

Oxford **MARYLAND**

Maryland seafood at its best

The Eastern Shore of Maryland is a peninsula triply blessed. Beneficiary of the Atlantic Ocean and Chesapeake Bay, its location has bestowed upon it a history vital to the founding of our country, a temperate climate, and a bountiful treasury of delicate seafoods.

The village of Oxford, founded in the mid-1660s, is located on the bayside of the peninsula, on the Tred Avon River. This particular piece of real estate was settled and civilized by the English because of a land grant from Lord Baltimore. A living remnant remains: the Oxford-Bellevue ferry, which started service in 1683. It still crosses the Tred Avon every day of the year. Next to the ferry, at water's edge, sits the Robert Morris Inn, which was constructed around 1710.

The inn began service as a private home occupied by British trade merchant Robert Morris. After a number of years it became a public house and inn, growing to three floors capped with a mansard roof. The original structure, which was built by ships' carpenters and has wooden pegged paneling, handhewn beams, and a beautiful enclosed staircase, thrives under the loving care of innkeepers Ken and Wendy Gibson. Though the Gibsons keep the inn much the way it has been over the past two centuries, they work to offer contemporary comforts to today's weary traveler. Rather than simply offering the collection of large rooms and tiny chambers original to the inn, they have carefully converted the smallest of the inn's bedrooms into charming two-room suites, all the while preserving the building's rich flavor of antiquity.

Next to history and atmosphere, people most enjoy the high quality of the regional fare served in the Robert Morris's three dining rooms. Its vaunted Maryland crabcakes are a house specialty that were given the highest marks in an article authored by long-time guest and crabcake expert, James Michener.

Left, top, the main dining room has four large antique murals made of rare hand-blocked wallpaper. *Bottom*, Room 1 is one of the largest guest rooms, with a view of the river and ferry. *Previous pages*, the Robert Morris Inn, on the Tred Avon River.

Room 15 on third floor, with old-fashioned steps.

The generous Robert Morris Seafood Platter includes chilled gulf shrimp and crabmeat, a crabcake, deep-fried shrimp and scallops, broiled seafood imperial, stuffed shrimp, a fish filet, *plus* a special seafood surprise! The inn dining rooms range from the fairly formal, with woodcut wall murals illuminated by crystal chandeliers, to a relaxed and pub-like atmosphere.

ROBERT MORRIS INN, P.O. Box 70, Oxford, MD 21654; (301) 226-5111; Kenneth and Wendy Gibson, Innkeepers. Rates: *moderate*. Open all year except at Christmas and mid-January to mid-March; 10 rooms with private baths; 6 rooms with shared baths. Restaurant open daily serving 3 meals to guests and public; bar serves liquor. Children 10 years and over welcome; no pets; separate dining rooms and guest rooms for smokers; major credit cards accepted. Nearby bicycle rental, tennis, boat rental, swimming, fishing.

DIRECTIONS: from Easton, follow Rte. 333 to the end, about 6 miles. The inn is on the right.

WHITE SWAN TAVERN

Chestertown   **MARYLAND**

Restored with extraordinary care

A short distance from the banks of the broad Chester River, on the main street of historic Chestertown, sits an inn which dates back to the early 1700s, when the village flourished. At the White Swan Tavern, guests feel that they've arrived at a special place. There is a sense of the extraordinary care that has gone into the restoration of this interesting building. As a result it feels fresh, immaculate, and solid as a rock.

The inn is tiny; its contains only five rooms, each spotlessly maintained. Two of the grandest rooms are the rustic John Lovegrove Kitchen, in which rough hewn structural posts are exposed and the large brick hearth neatly reconstructed, and the T.W. Eliason Suite, named after the last owner of the tavern who became Kent County's first millionaire. This latter two-room suite is furnished with antique period pieces; its intriguing blend of colors—moss green, copper, peach, and shades of cream and tan—recreate a soft Victorian mood. Upon arrival at the inn, guests find a large, chilled bottle of wine in their room. Later, they enjoy relaxing in the King Joseph Room, an inviting private parlor on the first floor that is filled with comfortable traditional furnishings, a tele-

Tea Time.

vision, books, and games. Congenial innkeeper Mary Clarkson arranges for breakfast to be brought to your door, if you like, and a satisfying tea is served daily in the Isaac Cannell room—a particularly attractive chamber furnished with Windsor chairs, game tables, and colonial artifacts.

WHITE SWAN TAVERN, 231 High Street, Chestertown, MD 21620; (301) 778-2300; Mary S. Clarkson, Innkeeper. Rates: *moderate,* including continental breakfast with freshly squeezed juices. Open all year except 3 weeks at the end of January into mid-February; 5 rooms, 2 suites, all with private baths. No restaurant or bar, complimentary wine in room. Children welcome; Spanish and French spoken; no credit cards accepted. Nearby golf, tennis, swimming, boat rentals, fishing, waterfowl hunting.

DIRECTIONS: from Chesapeake Bay Bridge (Rte. 50/301), take Rte. 301N to Rte. 213. Turn left on Rte. 213 to Chestertown, approx. 15 miles. Cross the Chester River Bridge and turn left at first stop light (Cross St.). Turn left again at next light (High St.). Inn is in middle of block on right. Parking in rear.

Above, the Thomas Peacock Room has a romantic bonnet canopied bed. *Left,* the entrance to the White Swan is from the back, past the flower gardens.

ADMIRAL FELL INN

Baltimore **MARYLAND**

An authentic restoration on Baltimore's revitalized harbor

Baltimore is a city of neighborhoods and none is more welcoming, historic, and colorful than Fells Point. Its personality is layered and faceted; its atmosphere relaxed and pleasing. Considered to be "one of the largest colonial workingmen's communities in existence," Fells Point is listed on the National Register of Historic Places and retains an eighteenth-century character.

The perfect place to stay while enjoying a visit to Baltimore is The Admiral Fell Inn located at water's edge in Fells Point. Innkeeper and avid sailor Jim Widman fell in love with the site, which originally offered overnight accommodations to sailors, and he set about refurbishing what once was the old Anchorage Hotel.

The result is a congenial blend of old and new. The unassuming brick exterior was stripped of a century of soot but retains an age-softened patina. While guests check in at an antique partner's desk, they relax to the rhythmic ticking of an English grandfather clock made in 1810. The spacious lobby, furnished with comfortable groupings of chairs and

The library sitting room off the lobby.

sofas, adjoins a small carpeted library and an atrium that towers four stories to the ceiling skylight. Each guest room has individual style, and all are furnished with fine period reproductions. Jim strives for and succeeds in balancing the warm hospitality of a fine inn with services generally found only in first-class hotels.

A point of pride at The Admiral Fell is the dining room. Chef M. B. Eiring employs the best of many cuisines, and the results are good to look at and even better to eat. A sampling from her menu includes thin slices of rare beef marinated in sesame dressing and served with enoki mushrooms; spinach salad with walnuts and sweetbreads tossed with a warm bacon vinaigrette; Chesapeake cioppino; game hen served on a bed of wild rice and napped with an apricot brandy demiglace; and veal scallopini garnished with artichoke hearts, prosciutto, capers, and dressed with lemon butter.

Above, afternoon tea in the lounge. *Left*, a classic 1920 mahogany yacht, the Sakonnet, can be chartered from the Admiral Fell, shown in the background. *Overleaf*, the inn is situated in Fell's Point, a charmingly restored part of Baltimore's waterfront.

THE ADMIRAL FELL INN, 888 South Broadway, Baltimore, MD 21231; (301) 522-7377 or (800) 292–4667; Jim Widman, Innkeeper. Rates: *moderate* and *expensive*, including continental breakfast and free van transportation in city. Open all year; 37 rooms, including 1 suite, all with private baths. Restaurant and pub open daily for lunch and dinner. Children welcome; major credit cards accepted. Located on Baltimore's historic waterfront; close to Aquarium, museums, arts, shopping.

DIRECTIONS: call for easiest directions to Fells Point.

INN AT BUCKEYSTOWN

Buckeystown　　　　　　　　　　　　　　　　**MARYLAND**

Dan's collection of Indian memorabilia.

Lively conversation and culinary treats

"What to do when the world falls apart: celebrations and feasts." Poring over innkeeper Dan Pelz's record of past menus one stumbles upon reflections that bespeak the caring philosophy and spirit which infuse The Inn at Buckeystown. Here, guests become members of an extended family, a family that enjoys good food, lively conversation, and the comforts of a fine old turn-of-the-century home.

Dan and co-innkeeper Marty Martinez discovered this stately mansion, one of the finest homes in the quiet village of Buckeystown, and immediately fell in love with its spaciousness, elegant lines, and lustrous chestnut woodwork. The house enjoys a spacious wraparound veranda on which guests savor the pure pleasures of reading, rocking, and just plain relaxing. Each evening at 6:30, the porch, or one of the comfortable inside parlors, becomes a meeting place for the before dinner apéritif. The inn takes on a glow during this early evening hour, and by 7:00 Dan is ready to display his culinary skills. Though he is especially proud of his homemade soups and fresh salads, each dish is prepared with skill and creativity. Dinner may consist of cream of lemon soup, a lightly-dressed salad of romaine, cantaloupe, and jumbo shrimp, savory osso bucco, garlic-buttered pasta, fresh green beans, and pineapple fool for dessert. A thoughtfully chosen wine accompanies the meal, which is served family style on antique china, crystal, and silver. Dan and Marty also love to mount elaborate theme dinners. Some of the most successful include their Pennsylvania Dutch Celebration, a California Summer Supper, an 1860s Regimental Dinner, and a lavish New Year's Day spread complete with oysters on the half shell, rabbit pâté, goose with gooseberry glaze, wild rice, and deep-dish blueberry pie.

Dan is an inverterate collector specializing in colorful images of clowns and American Indians, as well as antique lamps and furnishings. His collections, along with a wonderful selection of interesting magazines and books, are spread evenly throughout the inn. The guest bedrooms are romantic and very comfortable, the most luxurious being the Fireplace Room which resides at the front of the house and has a working fireplace, Victorian velvet tufted settee, a brocade slipper chair, a crystal chandelier, and a bay window overlooking the quiet, tree-shrouded street.

Above, one of the two parlors at the inn. *Left*, the inn, shaded by ancient trees, *top*, and a guest room, *bottom*, aptly named the Fireplace Room.

THE INN AT BUCKEYSTOWN, Buckeystown, MD 21717; (301) 874-5755; Daniel R. Pelz and Marty Martinez, Innkeepers. Rates: *moderate,* modified American plan with full breakfast and dinner included. Closed last 2 weeks in January and last 2 weeks in July; 8 rooms, shared baths. Dining room serves 2 meals daily to guests and public; complimentary wine with meals. Not suitable for children; no pets; no smoking in dining room; Visa, MasterCard and personal checks, accepted. Innkeepers are "game nuts". Victorian yard games, reading material, recreational facilities nearby including white-water rafting.

DIRECTIONS: the inn is 5miles south of Frederick, Md., on Rte. 85.

New Market # STRAWBERRY INN **MARYLAND**

Surrounded by 45 antiques shops

Although the Strawberry Inn is a small guest house, visitors sense a largeness about the place; it reflects the mood of the entire village of New Market, and vice versa. The inn sits directly on the Main Street of tiny New Market, a village on the National Register of Historic Places that has never been touched by commercialism. To find a supermarket, or even a gas station, one must venture outside of town. Many of the Federal-style private homes that line up neatly along the uneven brick sidewalk of Main Street serve as antiques shops; they number an astonishing forty-five in the one-mile stretch that makes up the town. Among these, the Strawberry Inn is an inviting white clapboard, green shuttered cottage which emanates a feeling of calm and quiet.

Innkeepers Ed and Jane Rossig chose to live in New Market in the early seventies because of its old-fashioned atmosphere, favorable climate, and because Ed wanted to restore this 1840s farm-style house. New Market's remarkable cache of antique shops was established in the 1930s, yet comfortable lodgings for overnight guests had never been available. After restoring the house, the Rossigs discovered the town was zoned strictly for antique shops *and* guest houses. Upon the urging of various antique dealers and visitors, they opened their doors to overnight visitors in 1973.

The inn is furnished with antiques, many of them family heirlooms. The 1776 Room, located on the

first floor, has two twin pineapple four-posters, a small loveseat, and various chests and chairs, every piece of which has been in Ed's family for generations. This room also opens onto a private porch—a wonderful spot for an alfresco breakfast during clement weather. The remaining guest rooms are located upstairs, and they range in size and spirit from the cozy 1865 Room, with its old iron and brass bed matched with an antique crocheted coverlet and soft maize and cream décor, to the Strawberry Room which contains a queen-size brass bed, an ornate Victorian brass floor lamp with hand-painted glass globe, and old-fashioned rose-patterned wallpaper.

Above, Jane and Ed Rossig, innkeepers for over a decade. *Left,* the 1776 Room has a private porch—wonderful for breakfast.

STRAWBERRY INN, (17 Main Street), P.O. Box 237, New Market, MD 21774; (301) 865-3318; Jane and Ed Rossig, Innkeepers, Rates: *inexpensive* and *moderate,* including continental breakfast with fresh-baked breads. Open all year; 5 rooms with private baths; meeting room available. No restaurant or bar, bring your own liquor. Children over 12 welcome; no pets; no credit cards accepted. Nearby tennis courts, golf, antiques shops all along Main Street (most closed Mondays).

DIRECTIONS: from Frederick, Maryland, take I-70 east about 7 miles to exit 60. Follow signs to New Market. Inn is on Main Street.

VIRGINIA

RED FOX TAVERN

An historic inn in the heart of hunt country

When Joseph Chinn opened his sturdy stone tavern in 1728, he couldn't have foreseen that Chinn's Ordinary was destined to be as popular in the twentieth century as it was with his fellow colonists. In Chinn's day young George Washington, then a staunch royalist, passed through the tavern portals on his way to becoming the father of our country. A century later Confederate General J.E.B. Stuart planned strategy with the leader of the famous Mounted Rangers, Colonel John Mosby, in the private second-floor dining room. John F. Kennedy held a press conference in that same room some one hundred years later, and his wife, Jacqueline, who loved this rolling hunt country, was a frequent patron of the inn. By the mid-1970s the property, now known as The Red Fox Tavern, came into the loving hands of the Reuter family, who have spent the last decade and-a-half restoring, polishing, and enlarging what is today the Red Fox complex.

The main inn completely retains its colonial character and the genteel charm of days gone by, but has been made comfortable with the welcome addition of twentieth-century amenities. Several doors away is the Stray Fox Inn, a rambling buttercream yellow

The Stray Fox Inn is an aptly named addition to the Red Fox.

stucco guest house built in the early 1800s. Rooms in this attractive annex range from the grand and spacious Belmont Suite to the Furness Suite at the top of the house (particularly suited for honeymooners). Across the lane is the newly restored McConnell House, with three single rooms and two suites.

An especially nice feature new to the Red Fox is the wide variety of dining options available to guests. The tavern serves three meals a day with the dinner menu featuring a well-wrought selection of appetizers, entrées, and desserts. But if you're seeking a more casual, lighter menu the Reuters recently opened Mosby's Tavern in a neighboring building. Here you can find anything from beef empanadas and Brunswick stew to pizza and prime rib. On weekends you might even find a d.j. spinning discs to dance to.

Above, the Jefferson Davis Room, one of the original bedrooms in the main inn. *Left*, the centuries-old craft of making interesting and charming inn signs survives into the present day, as evidenced at the Red Fox. *Previous page*, a second-floor dining room in marvelous wood paneling at the Red Fox Tavern.

THE RED FOX TAVERN, (2 East Washington Street), P.O. Box 385, Middleburg, VA 22117; (703) 687-6301; Turner and Dana Reuter, Innkeepers. Rates: *moderate* and *expensive,* with continental breakfast. Open all year; 17 rooms, including suites, in McConnell House, Old Tavern, Stray Fox, all with private baths. Restaurant open 7 days for 3 meals a day; Sunday, country breakfast and dinner, for guests and public; bar serves late night menu to 11:30 P.M. Children welcome; no pets, but kennel service available with advance notice; some French and Spanish spoken; all major credit cards accepted. Occasional live entertainment at Mosby's; Luray Caverns, Skyline Drive, Harper's Ferry day trips.

DIRECTIONS: from east take Rte. 66 west to Dulles/Winchester exit onto Rte. 50 west and go approx. 20 miles to center of Middleburg. Inn at right corner on blinking light. Register in tavern. From west, take I-81 and exit onto Rte. 50 east at Winchester and drive approx. 30 miles to Middleburg.

INN AT LITTLE WASHINGTON

Washington

VIRGINIA

Glowingly reviewed by gourmets

A diner at the adjoining table, a restauranteur as it happened, literally hummed and sang with pleasure at the arrival of each new course. After making short work of a plate of fresh foie gras, smoked goose breast, and local country ham, served on a bed of black-eyed peas vinaigrette, followed by a charcoal grilled veal tenderloin with rosemary cream, he could no longer contain himself. "This fellow creates dishes

A sherbet sampler as delicious as it is strikingly beautiful.

I've never tasted before in my life. I must say that this is the best meal I've ever had anywhere."

A growing group of gourmets are drawing the same conclusion at The Inn at Little Washington. As pilgrims to the inn proliferate, the word is spreading that chef Patrick O'Connell and innkeeper/partner Reinhardt Lynch are artists in the pursuit of creating

Left, a before-dinner hors d'oeuvre of smoked trout with watercress mayonaise, and prawns with dill mayonaise and red peppers. *Below*, the main dining room, where a buffet breakfast is offered along with a full breakfast of cooked-to-order dishes.

one of those very rare American inns truly "worth a detour."

The inn's beginnings in the late 1970s did not bespeak coming grandeur. After operating a successful catering business Pat and Reinhardt opened a small restaurant in a nondescript building in the center of Washington, Virginia, a lovely country village tucked into the foothills of the Blue Ridge Mountains. Eventually a glowing review, which also mentioned the relative discomfort of local overnight accommodations, came from a Washington, D.C. food critic. The seed was sown both for a growing, far-flung following as well as a clutch of luxurious, private, and beautifully appointed guest rooms.

The inn attracts the sophisticated traveler who appreciates the art of fine living. A certain degree of understatement plays an essential role at the inn. No signpost alerts the passerby that this is an inn, *the* inn. One and all must ring the doorbell to gain entry. Once inside, privacy, quiet, elegance, and attention from a well-mannered and gracious staff combine to make this inn a haven.

The dining room and adjoining garden are har-

Below, the private garden at night. *Opposite page*, Room 7, showing leaded-glass privacy door that adds extra soundproofing.

monious spaces that combine English-American style and a measure of Oriental simplicity. The innkeepers commissioned a renowned lighting expert to create the glow of the full moon in the nighttime garden. The dining room is illuminated by light reflected through rich peach taffeta lampshades, and the glow is romantic and magical. The scene is set for Patrick's seasonal delights, which may include marinated shiitake mushrooms on vermicelli, fricasse of lobster with apples and Calvados, and a luscious sampler of fresh fruit sherbets.

THE INN AT LITTLE WASHINGTON, Washington, VA 22747; (703) 675-3800; Patrick O'Connell and Reinhardt Lynch, Innkeepers. Rates: *expensive*, including full breakfast. Open all year; 8 rooms and 2 penthouse suites, all with private baths, penthouse suites with Jacuzzis. Restaurant open Wednesday–Sunday for dinner only, for guests and public; lounge serves liquor. Children over 10; no pets; Visa and Mastercard accepted. Hiking, tennis, Shenandoah National Park, antiques shops nearby.

DIRECTIONS: from Washington, D.C. take I-66 west and drive 28 miles to exit 10A. Take 29 south 12 miles to Warrenton; turn right at Howard Johnson's onto Rte. 211 west and drive 23 miles. Turn right at Washington sign. Inn is ½ mile on right at crossroads of Middle and Main Streets.

Southern hospitality from a native New Yorker

First-time guests at this genteel plantation mansion might expect a soft-spoken Southern gentleman to greet them at the door, mint julep in hand. Instead they meet spirited, likable—and gentlemanly—Bill Sheehan, a native New Yorker who is passionate about innkeeping, preparing delicious food, and restoring vintage cars.

The oldest section of the inn dates to 1732, the year when Roger Thompson was forced to convert the barn on his property into a dwelling after a fire had destroyed his home. Over a century later, William Overton bought the property, increased the land to nearly 1600 acres, and planted a wonderful sampling of trees, including a rare magnolia macrofilia and varieties of poplar, beech, hemlock, ash, maple, and locust. After the Civil War Overton's son began taking in city guests, and the family's home became an inn. Today the inn is part of the Green Springs National Historic District, and one of thirteen eighteenth-century plantations, each unspoiled and unchanged. Bill and wife Mireille fell in love with the romance of Prospect Hill and adopted this Virginia landmark as their home.

The focal point of any stay at Prospect Hill is dinner. In keeping with Mireille's French heritage the inn celebrates the savory pleasures of the table, and Bill's kitchen issues forth deftly prepared, delicious French dishes.

The Sheehans offer overnight accommodations in the plantation house and in a row of historic buildings that run between the house and the large swimming pool. The out cottages, named after their original residents—Overseers Cottage, The Boy's Cabin, Uncle Guy's Cabin—vary in size and atmosphere. The smallest accommodation, The Boy's Cabin, is the perfect nook for honeymooners or romantics of any ilk. Rough-hewn plank and mortar walls weave a cozy spell, and a small porch at the back overlooks the pool. Rooms in the house are antiques-filled and old-fashioned and range from a grand, two-room suite in the oldest section to a diminutive chamber furnished with a simple pineapple four-poster bed and a wardrobe, wing chair, and vanity.

Above, one of three decorative dining rooms. *Left*, spring garden vegetable consommé, one of Bill Sheehan's specialties. *Overleaf*, guests enjoy a complimentary aperitif on the spacious lawn.

PROSPECT HILL, Rte. 613, Trevilians, VA 23170; (703) 967-0844; Mireille and Bill Sheehan, Innkeepers, Melvin Henson, Manager. Rates: *moderate*, including full breakfast; dinner included in rates Wednesday to Saturday. Open all year except Christmas eve and Christmas day; 3 rooms in main house, 4 in former slave quarters, all with private baths. Restaurant serves breakfast daily for guests only and dinner Wednesday to Saturday for guests and public; wine, beer, aperitifs served. Children welcome but not recommended; no pets; smoking, but allergic guests will be accommodated; French spoken; Visa, MasterCard, and personal checks accepted. Swimming in pool, golf at Monticello, canoeing on Rivanna River, historical sightseeing, antiquing, country auctions.

DIRECTIONS: the inn is 15 miles east of Charlottesville, Va. From Richmond or Charlottesville take I-64 to exit 27 onto Rte. 15 south ½ mile to Zion Crossroads. Turn left on Rte. 250 east 1 mile to Rte. 613 and turn left. Inn is on left 3 miles down.

SILVER THATCH INN

Charlottesville · **VIRGINIA**

Veal and lobster in brandy cream; swordfish baked with Champagne . . .

When Shelley and Tim Dwight met in Atlantic City, they were working in a large hotel casino, Tim in management and Shelley in the kitchen. With this combined experience, they decided to leave the bright lights behind and strike out on their own. They searched the mid-Atlantic states and found their inn, a rambling, but tidy colonial cottage, which, today, is known as the Silver Thatch.

Because of Shelley's culinary efforts, the Silver Thatch is becoming known as one of the best dining rooms in the Charlottesville area. Her seasonal menus tend toward country French cuisine, and past dishes have included sautéed, boneless breast of chicken topped with mushrooms, tomatoes, and demiglace; veal and lobster in brandy cream sauce; swordfish baked with champagne and lime butter; and filet mignon stuffed with herbed spinach purée and napped with garlic cream. Shelley excels in preparing satisfying appetizers and soups, such as delicious Black Forest soup that blends escargots, truffles, herbs, and a touch of pernod; mushroom caps filled with cheese, bacon, and herbs; and capellini, Canadian bacon, and shrimp bathed in a light cream sauce and topped with red caviar.

The inn's first floor comprises three dining rooms and a small and cozy tavern. Two of these rooms are decorated with simple, traditional furnishings, the English Room with its Federal fireplace and elegant wallpaper being the more formal of the two. The third chamber, the Hessian Room, dates back to 1780, making it one of the oldest buldings in this part of Virginia. The room is named after its builders, captive Hessian solders, who, after being taken prisoner at the battle of Saratoga, were marched south to Charlottesville. The exposed, rustic beams and rough plaster walls of the original two-story structure create a rich aura of colonial America. The second floor of this section is a guest room with irregular eaves, deep-set windows, and comfortable furnishings.

Elsewhere in the inn are several other guest rooms, each with its own personality. The largest room, named after Thomas Jefferson, has as its centerpiece a four-poster bed with a fishnet canopy.

Above, the Thomas Jefferson Room is the inn's most spacious guest room. *Left*, the English Room, set up for elegant dining.

SILVER THATCH INN, 3001 Hollymead Drive, Charlottesville, VA 22901; (804) 978-4686; Tim and Shelley Dwight, Innkeepers. Rates: *moderate*, including continental breakfast. Closed first 2 weeks in January; 7 rooms, 4 in main building and 3 in separate cottage, all with private baths. Dining room open Tuesday through Saturday serving dinner to guests and public. Bar serves liquor. Not ideal for small children; no pets; major credit cards accepted. Swimming pool and tennis courts; Monticello, Ashlawn, University of Virginia, Skyline Drive nearby.

DIRECTIONS: from Richmond take I-64 west to exit 25. Turn right onto Rte. 250 west which becomes 250 West Bypass. Take 250 W. Bypass to Rte. 29 north and drive 5 miles. Turn right at Rte. 1520, at sign for inn. From Skyline Drive take Rte. 250 east to Rte. 29 north in Charlottesville. Drive 5 miles and turn right at inn sign.

Warm Springs MEADOW LANE LODGE

Hundreds of acres of heaven in Virginia

Near the inn is the Garth Newel Music Center, for which the Hirshes had this wonderful harpsichord made. Director Luca Di Cecco is standing in the background.

Cathy and Philip Hirsh's sixteen hundred acres of Virginia mountain meadow land are a world removed. Guests enter the property via a long and secluded lane which opens onto a simple yet spectacular country hideaway. The property has been in the Hirsh family for generations, and it has that special atmosphere particular to a place long-cherished and cared for. Guests at the inn stay in the Lodge, a charming clapboard farmhouse, or in an adjoining separate cottage close to the Lodge. One and all make use of the Lodge's inviting common room which is flanked by two large fieldstone fireplaces and filled with family heirlooms and a great selection of books and magazines. No guest room at Meadow Lane is quite like any other, however, all are quintessentially charming, simple, antiques-filled, and comfortable.

Each morning Philip prepares breakfast for his guests, a magnificent repast served in the Lodge's sunny conservatory and watched over by an oil portrait of his father, who, incidentally, was the author of Yale College's famed chant, "Boola-boola." Combining an appreciation for interesting tastes and textures with a nostalgia for great breakfasts from

his childhood, Phip might serve up shirred eggs nested in a savory blend of sausage and spiced apples, veal hash with Bordeaux sauce, popovers, poached finnan haddie, fried grits with maple syrup, or kippered herring.

The meadows surrounding the inn are populated with a veritable grazing zoo. Horses, donkeys, black and white Nubian goats, peacocks, guinea fowl, pigeons, turkeys, geese, cats, and dogs gambol about in peaceful harmony. After touring this free-ranging menagerie one might play tennis, relax by the swimming pool, hike one of the several trails (ranging from easy to strenuous), or angle for trout in the Jackson River, two miles of which flow through the Hirsh's property. In fact, the property is so blessed with this river and several clear spring-fed ponds that the famed Orvis Fishing School convenes sessions at Meadow Lane from May through October.

Left, innkeepers Cathy and Philip Hirsh, with their Jack Russell terriers and their daughter's Silkie chicken.

MEADOW LANE LODGE, Star Route A, Box 110, Warm Springs, VA 24484, (703) 839-5959; Philip and Catherine Hirsh, Innkeepers. Rates: *moderate*, including full breakfast. Open April 1 through January 1; 7 rooms plus Francisco Cottage in village, all with private baths. No restaurant or bar. Children welcome; pets with prior approval, must be leashed; all major credit cards accepted. Swimming, tennis, croquet, fishing, on premises. Golf, chamber music concerts, antiquing nearby.

DIRECTIONS: from Staunton, Va. take Rte. 254 west to Buffalo Gap and then Rte. 42 south to Millboro Springs and pick up Rte. 39 west to Warm Springs. From Roanoke take Rte. 220 north to Warm Springs and Rte. 39 west 4 miles to inn.

MARTHA WASHINGTON INN

Abingdon

VIRGINIA

Antiques original to the inn fill many of the guest rooms.

Luxurious amenities on a grand scale

The Martha Washington Inn is a venerable Federalist landmark building, constructed in 1832 as a private home for General Francis Preston, a Virginia Congressman and officer in the War of 1812. From 1858 until 1932, the building served as the Martha Washington College for young women and in 1935 was converted to an inn. By the early 1980s, it was undergoing a renaissance, her grand salons and many bedrooms slowly receiving new coats of paint and being filled with refurbished antiques.

Today the proud recipient of a complete—and very expensive—facelift, The Martha Washington Inn is a first-class inn/hotel, having no peer for many miles around. The main entry hall is dominated by a large, black marble banker's table with ormolu mounts and Empire legs, an antique crystal chandelier, and a series of twenty-four original *Scenes of America* done in 1835 by French artist Dufour. Four formal parlors flank the entrance and are furnished with pedigree antiques restored to a gleaming finish.

The many guest rooms in the main building and in two attached wings are totally renovated and rival accommodations in the finest hotels. Most contain at least a smattering of antiques original to The Martha, amidst a sensitive blend of good reproduction and traditional pieces.

The menu in The Martha's elegant dining room, First Lady's Table, offers a wide selection of seafoods, meats, poultry, pasta, and salads. Each Friday night the chef prepares a popular seafood buffet with a bounty of fresh fish flown in from the coast. The famous Barter Theater, founded during the Depression when hungry actors bartered acting for farm produce, sits adjacent to the inn, and The Martha's pre-theater buffets allow one to satisfy a dual appetite for food and art.

Left, teatime on the porch, served by Pete Scheffey. *Overleaf*, the dining room is grand and spacious.

THE MARTHA WASHINGTON INN, 150 West Main Street, Abingdon, VA 24210; (703) 628-3161; Jim Watts, General Manager. Rates: *moderate* and *expensive*. Open all year; 61 standard rooms, deluxe rooms, and suites, all with private baths, some with Jacuzzis, some with steam rooms. Dining room serves 3 meals daily, including Friday seafood buffet and Sunday brunch, for guests and public; 2 bars and live entertainment. No pets; all major credit cards accepted. Golf, tennis, swimming, Barter Theater (April to October), antiques and specialty shops nearby.

DIRECTIONS: from Roanoke, Va., or from Knoxville, Tenn., take I-81 to exit 8 (Abingdon); drive 1 mile into town and turn right on Main Street. Inn is on the right.